THE HYMNS OF FRANCES RIDLEY HAVERGAL

The *Hymns* of FRANCES RIDLEY HAVERGAL

COMPLIED BY
CHARLES J. DOE

CURIOSMITH
MINNEAPOLIS

Published by Curiosmith.
P. O. Box 390293, Minneapolis, Minnesota, 55439.
Internet: curiosmith.com.
E-mail: shopkeeper@curiosmith.com.

Scripture quotations are from the *Holy Bible*, King James Version.

ISBN 9781946145314

CONTENTS

FIRST LINE

ANOTHER YEAR

ANOTHER year is dawning!
  Dear Master, let it be,
In working or in waiting,
  Another year with Thee.

Another year of leaning
  Upon Thy loving breast,
Of ever-deepening trustfulness,
  Of quiet, happy rest.

Another year of mercies,
  Of faithfulness and grace;
Another year of gladness
  In the shining of Thy face.

Another year of progress,
  Another year of praise;
Another year of proving
  Thy presence "all the days."

Another year of service,
  Of witness for Thy love;
Another year of training
  For holier work above.

Another year is dawning,
  Dear Master, let it be,
On earth, or else in heaven,
  Another year for Thee!

DAILY STRENGTH

"As thy day thy strength shall be!"
This should be enough for thee;
He who knows thy frame will spare
Burdens more than thou canst bear.

When thy days are veiled in night,
Christ shall give thee heavenly light;
Seem they wearisome and long,
Yet in Him thou shalt be strong.

Cold and wintry though they prove,
Thine the sunshine of His love,
Or, with fervid heat oppressed,
In His shadow thou shalt rest.

When thy days on earth are past,
Christ shall call thee home at last,
His redeeming love to praise,
Who hath strengthened all thy days.

THE TRIUNE PRESENCE

(BIRTHDAY OR NEW YEAR'S HYMN)

Certainly I will be with thee.—Exodus 3:12.

"CERTAINLY I will be with thee!" Father, I have found it true:
To Thy faithfulness and mercy I would set my seal anew.
All the year Thy grace hath kept me, Thou my help indeed hast been,
Marvellous the loving-kindness every day and hour hath seen.

"Certainly I will be with thee!" Let me feel it, Saviour dear,
Let me know that Thou art with me, very precious, very near.
On this day of solemn pausing, with Thyself all longing still,
Let Thy pardon, let Thy presence, let Thy peace my spirit fill.

"Certainly I will be with thee!" Blessed Spirit, come to me,
Rest upon me, dwell within me, let my heart Thy temple be;
Through the trackless year before me, Holy One, with me abide!
Teach me, comfort me, and calm me, be my ever-present Guide.

"Certainly I will be with thee!" Starry promise in the night!
All uncertainties, like shadows, flee away before its light.
"Certainly I will be with thee!" He hath spoken: I have heard!
True of old, and true this moment, I will trust Jehovah's word.

SANCTIFIED

Sanctified in Christ Jesus.—1 Corinthians 1:2.

CHURCH of God, beloved and chosen, Church of Christ, for whom He died,
Claim thy gifts and praise thy Giver!—*"Ye are washed and sanctified."*
Sanctified by God the Father, and by Jesus Christ His Son,
And by God the Holy Spirit, Holy, Holy Three in One.

By His will He sanctifieth, by the Spirit's power within;
By the loving Hand that chasteneth fruits of righteousness to win;
By His truth and by His promise, by the Word, His gift unpriced,
By His own blood, and by union with the risen life of Christ.

Holiness by faith in Jesus, not by effort of thine own,—
Sin's dominion crushed and broken by the power of grace alone,—
God's own holiness within thee, His own beauty on thy brow,—
This shall be thy pilgrim brightness, this thy blessed portion now.

He will sanctify thee wholly; body, spirit, soul shall be
Blameless till thy Saviour's coming in His glorious majesty!
He hath perfected for ever those whom He hath sanctified;
Spotless, glorious, and holy is the Church, His chosen Bride.

FOR NEW YEAR'S DAY, 1874

From glory to glory.—2 Corinthians 3:18.

"FROM glory unto glory!" Be this our joyous song,
As on the King's own highway we bravely march along!
"From glory unto glory!" O word of stirring cheer,
As dawns the solemn brightness of another glad New Year.

Our own beloved Master "hath many things to say;"
Look forward to His teaching, unfolding day by day;
To whispers of His Spirit, while resting at His feet,
To glowing revelation, to insight clear and sweet.

"From glory unto glory!" Our faith hath seen the King,
We own His matchless beauty, as adoringly we sing:
But He hath more to show us! O thought of untold bliss!
And we press on exultingly in certain hope to this:—

To marvellous outpourings of His "treasures new and old,"
To largess of His bounty, paid in the King's own gold,
To glorious expansion of His mysteries of grace,
To radiant unveilings of the brightness of His face.

"From glory unto glory!" What great things He hath done,
What wonders He hath shown us, what triumphs He hath won!
We marvel at the records of the blessings of the year!
But sweeter than the Christmas bells rings out His promise clear—

That "greater things," far greater, our longing eyes shall see!
We can but wait and wonder what "greater things" shall be!
But glorious fulfilments rejoicingly we claim,
While pleading in the power of the All-prevailing Name.

"From glory unto glory!" What mighty blessings crown
The lives for which our Lord hath laid His own so freely down!
Omnipotence to keep us, Omniscience to guide,
Jehovah's Triune Presence within us to abide!

The fulness of His blessing encompasseth our way;
The fulness of His promises crowns every brightening day;
The fulness of His glory is beaming from above,
While more and more we realize the fulness of His love.

"From glory unto glory!" Without a shade of care,
Because the Lord who loves us will every burden bear;
Because we trust Him fully, and know that He will guide,
And know that He will keep us at His beloved side.

"From glory unto glory!" Though tribulation fall,
It cannot touch our treasure, when Christ is all in all!
Whatever lies before us, there can be naught to fear,
For what are pain and sorrow when Jesus Christ is near?

"From glory unto glory!" O marvels of the word!
"With open face beholding the glory of the Lord,"
We, even we (O wondrous grace!) "are changed into the same,"
The image of our Saviour, to glorify His Name.

Abiding in His presence, and walking in the light,
And seeking to "do always what is pleasing in His sight,"
We look to Him to keep us "all glorious within,"
Because "the blood of Jesus Christ *is cleansing* from all sin."

The things behind forgetting, we only gaze before,
"From glory unto glory," that "shineth more and more,"
Because our Lord hath said it, that such shall be our way
(O splendour of the promise!) "unto the perfect day."

"From glory unto glory!" Our fellow-travellers still
Are gathering on the journey! the bright electric thrill
Of quick instinctive union, more frequent and more sweet,
Shall swiftly pass from heart to heart in true and tender beat.

And closer yet, and closer the golden bonds shall be,
Enlinking all who love our Lord in pure sincerity;
And wider yet, and wider shall the circling glory glow,
As more and more are taught of God that mighty love to know.

O ye who seek the Saviour, look up in faith and love,
Come up into the sunshine, so bright and warm above!
No longer tread the valley, but, clinging to His hand,
Ascend the shining summits and view the glorious land.

Our harp-notes should be sweeter, our trumpet-tones more clear,
Our anthems ring so grandly, that all the world must hear!
Oh, royal be our music, for who hath cause to sing
Like the chorus of redeemed ones, the Children of the King!

Oh, let our adoration for all that He hath done
Peal out beyond the stars of God, while voice and life are one!
And let our consecration be real, and deep, and true;
Oh, even now our hearts shall bow, and joyful vows renew!—

"In full and glad surrender we give ourselves to Thee,
Thine utterly, and only, and evermore to be!
O Son of God, who lovest us, we will be Thine alone,
And all we are, and all we have, shall henceforth be Thine own!"

Now, onward, ever onward, from "strength to strength" we go,
While "grace for grace" abundantly shall from His fulness flow,
To glory's full fruition, from glory's foretaste here,
Until His Very Presence crown our happiest New Year!

THE SOVEREIGNTY OF GOD

Be still, and know that I am God.—Psalm 46:10.

GOD Almighty! King of nations! earth Thy footstool, heaven Thy throne!
Thine the greatness, power, and glory,Thine the kingdom, Lord, alone!
Life and death are in Thy keeping, and Thy will ordaineth all,
From the armies of Thy heavens to an unseen insect's fall.

Reigning, guiding, all-commanding, ruling myriad worlds of light;
Now exalting, now abasing, none can stay Thy hand of might!
Working all things by Thy power, by the counsel of Thy will,
Thou art God! enough to know it, and to hear Thy word: "Be still!"

In Thy sovereignty rejoicing, we Thy children bow and praise,
For we know that kind and loving, just and true, are all Thy ways.
While Thy heart of sovereign mercy and Thine arm of sovereign might,
For our great and strong salvation, in Thy sovereign grace unite.

WAIT PATIENTLY FOR HIM

GOD doth not bid thee wait
To disappoint at last;
A golden promise, fair and great,
In precept-mould is cast.
Soon shall the morning gild
The dark horizon-rim,
Thy heart's desire shall be fulfilled,
"*Wait* patiently for Him."

The weary waiting times
Are but the muffled peals
Low preluding celestial chimes,
That hail His chariot-wheels.
Trust Him to tune thy voice
To blend with seraphim;
His "Wait" shall issue in "Rejoice!"
"Wait *patiently* for Him."

He doth not bid thee wait,
Like drift-wood on the wave,
For fickle chance or fixed fate
To ruin or to save.
Thine eyes shall surely see,
No distant hope or dim,
The Lord thy God arise for thee:
"Wait patiently *for Him.*"

THY KINGDOM COME

GOD of heaven! hear our singing;
    Only little ones are we,
Yet a great petition bringing,
    Father, now we come to Thee.

Let Thy kingdom come, we pray Thee,
    Let the world in Thee find rest;
Let all know Thee, and obey Thee,
    Loving, praising, blessing, blessed!

Let the sweet and joyful story
    Of the Saviour's wondrous love,
Wake on earth a song of glory,
    Like the angel's song above.

Father, send the glorious hour,
    Every heart be Thine alone!
For the kingdom, and the power,
    And the glory are Thine own.

ALL

I.

GOD'S reiterated "ALL!"
  O wondrous word of peace and power!
TOUCHING with its tuneful fall
  THE rising of each hidden hour,
                    All the day.

II.

ONLY *all* His word believe,
  ALL peace and joy your heart shall fill,
ALL things asked ye shall receive:
  THIS is Thy Father's word and will,
                    For to-day.

III.

"*ALL* I have is thine," saith He.
  "*ALL* things are yours," He saith again;
ALL the promises for thee
  ARE sealed with Jesus Christ's Amen,
                    For to-day.

IV.

HE shall *all* your need supply,
  AND He will make *all* grace abound,
ALWAYS all sufficiency
  IN Him for *all* things shall be found,
                    For to-day.

V.

ALL His work He shall fulfil,
  ALL the good pleasure of His will,
KEEPING thee in *all* thy ways,
  AND with thee always, *"all* the days,"
                    And to-day!

ASCENSION SONG

He ascended up on high.—Ephesians 4:8.

GOLDEN harps are sounding,
　Angel voices ring,
Pearly gates are opened—
　Opened for the King;
Christ, the King of Glory,
　Jesus, King of Love,
Is gone up in triumph
　To His throne above.
　　All His work is ended,
　　Joyfully we sing,
　　Jesus hath ascended!
　　Glory to our King!

He who came to save us,
　He who bled and died,
Now is crowned with glory
　At His Father's side.
Never more to suffer,
　Never more to die
Jesus, King of Glory,
　Is gone up on high.
　　All His work is ended,
　　Joyfully we sing,
　　Jesus hath ascended!
　　Glory to our King!

Praying for His children,
　In that blessed place,
Calling them to glory,
　Sending them His grace;
His bright home preparing,
　Faithful ones, for you;
Jesus ever liveth,
　Ever loveth too.
　　All His work is ended,
　　Joyfully we sing,
　　Jesus hath ascended!
　　Glory to our King!

A HAPPY NEW YEAR

A HAPPY New Year! Oh such may it be!
Joyously, surely, and fully for thee!
Fear not and faint not, but be of good cheer,
And trustfully enter thy happy New Year!

Happy, so happy! Thy Father shall guide,
Protect thee, preserve thee, and always provide!
Onward and upward along the right way
Lovingly leading thee day by day.

Happy, so happy! Thy Saviour shall be
Ever more precious and present with thee!
Happy, so happy! His Spirit thy Guest,
Filling with glory the place of His rest.

Happy, so happy! Though shadows around
May gather and darken, they flee at the sound
Of the glorious Voice that saith, "Be of good cheer!"
Then joyously enter thy happy New Year!

HAVE YOU NOT A WORD FOR JESUS?

O Lord, open Thou my lips; and my mouth shall show forth Thy praise.
—Psalm 51:15.

HAVE you not a word for Jesus? not a word to say for Him?
He is listening through the chorus of the burning seraphim!
HE is LISTENING; does He hear you speaking of the things of earth,
Only of its passing pleasure, selfish sorrow, empty mirth?
He has spoken words of blessing, pardon, peace, and love to you,
Glorious hopes and gracious comfort, strong and tender, sweet and true;
Does He hear you telling others something of His love untold,
Overflowings of thanksgiving for His mercies manifold?

Have you not a word for Jesus? Will the world His praise proclaim?
Who shall speak if ye are silent? ye who know and love His name.
You, whom He hath called and chosen His own witnesses to be,
Will you tell your gracious Master, "Lord, we cannot speak for Thee"?
"Cannot!" though He suffered for you, died because He loved you so!
"Cannot!" though He has forgiven, making scarlet white as snow!
"Cannot!" though His grace abounding is your freely promised aid!
"Cannot!" though HE stands beside you, though HE says, "Be not afraid!"

Have you not a word for Jesus? Some, perchance, while ye are dumb,
Wait and weary for your message, hoping *you* will bid them "come";
Never telling hidden sorrows, lingering just outside the door,
Longing for *your* hand to lead them into rest for evermore.
Yours may be the joy and honour His redeemed ones to bring,
Jewels for the coronation of your coming Lord and King.
Will you cast away the gladness thus your Master's joy to share,
All because a word for Jesus seems too much for you to dare?

What shall be our word for Jesus? Master, give it day by day;
Ever as the need arises, teach Thy children what to say.
Give us holy love and patience; grant us deep humility,
That of self we may be emptied, and our hearts be full of Thee;
Give us zeal and faith and fervour, make us winning, make us wise,
Single-hearted, strong and fearless,—Thou hast called us, we will rise!
Let the might of Thy good Spirit go with every loving word;
And by hearts prepared and opened be our message always heard!

Yes, we have a word for Jesus! Living echoes we will be,
Of Thine own sweet words of blessing, of Thy gracious "Come to Me."
Jesus, Master! yes, we love Thee, and to prove our love, would lay
Fruit of lips which Thou wilt open, at Thy blessed feet to-day.
Many an effort it may cost us, many a heart-beat, many a fear,
But Thou knowest, and wilt strengthen, and Thy help is always near.
Give us grace to follow fully, vanquishing our faithless shame,
Feebly it may be, but truly, witnessing for Thy dear Name.

Yes, we have a word for Jesus! we will bravely speak for Thee,
And Thy bold and faithful soldiers, Saviour, we would henceforth be:
In Thy name set up our banners, while Thine own shall wave above,
With Thy crimson Name of Mercy, and Thy golden Name of Love.
Help us lovingly to labour, looking for Thy present smile,
Looking for Thy promised blessing, through the brightening "little while."
Words for Thee in weakness spoken, Thou wilt here accept and own,
And confess them in Thy glory, when we see Thee on Thy throne.

LISTENING IN DARKNESS–SPEAKING IN LIGHT

What I tell you in darkness, that speak ye in light.—Matthew 10:27

HE hath spoken in the darkness,
    In the silence of the night,
Spoken sweetly of the Father,
    Words of life and love and light.
Floating through the sombre stillness
    Came the loved and loving Voice,
Speaking peace and solemn gladness,
    That His children might rejoice.
What He tells thee in the darkness,
    Songs He giveth in the night—
Rise and speak it in the morning,
    Rise and sing them in the light!

He hath spoken in the darkness,
    In the silence of thy grief,
Sympathy so deep and tender,
    Mighty for thy heart relief;
Speaking in thy night of sorrow
    Words of comfort and of calm,
Gently on thy wounded spirit
    Pouring true and healing balm.
What He tells thee in the darkness,
    Weary watcher for the day,
Grateful lip and life should utter
    When the shadows flee away.

He is speaking in the darkness,
    Though thou canst not see His face,
More than angels ever needed,
    Mercy, pardon, love, and grace.
Speaking of the many mansions,
    Where, in safe and holy rest,
Thou shalt be with Him for ever,
    Perfectly and always blest.
What He tells thee in the darkness,
    Whispers through Time's lonely night,
Thou shalt speak in glorious praises,
    In the everlasting light!

FRESH SPRINGS

All my fresh springs shall be in Thee.—Psalm 87:7.
(Prayer-Book Version)

HEAR the Father's ancient promise!
　　Listen, thirsty, weary one!
"I will pour My Holy Spirit
　　On Thy chosen seed, O Son."
Promise to the Lord's Anointed,
　　Gift of God to Him for thee!
Now, by covenant appointed,
　　All thy springs in Him shall be.

Springs of life in desert places
　　Shall thy God unseal for thee;
Quickening and reviving graces,
　　Dew-like, healing, sweet and free.
Springs of sweet refreshment flowing,
　　When thy work is hard or long,
Courage, hope, and power bestowing,
　　Lightening labour with a song.

Springs of peace, when conflict heightens,
　　Thine uplifted eye shall see;
Peace that strengthens, calms, and brightens,
　　Peace itself a victory.
Springs of comfort, strangely springing,
　　Through the bitter wells of woe;
Founts of hidden gladness, bringing
　　Joy that earth can ne'er bestow.

Thine, O Christian, is this treasure,
　　To Thy risen Head assured!
Thine in full and gracious measure,
　　Thine by covenant secured!
Now arise! His word possessing,
　　Claim the promise of the Lord;
Plead through Christ for showers of blessing,
　　Till the Spirit be outpoured!

THE INFINITY OF GOD

Too wonderful for me.—Psalm 139:6.

HOLY and Infinite! Viewless, Eternal!
  Veiled in the glory that none can sustain,
None comprehendeth Thy being supernal,
  Nor can the heaven of heavens contain.

Holy and Infinite! limitless, boundless
  All Thy perfections, and power, and praise!
Ocean of mystery! awful and soundless
  All Thine unsearchable judgments and ways!

King of Eternity! what revelation
  Could the created and finite sustain,
But for Thy marvellous manifestation,
  Godhead incarnate in weakness and pain!

Therefore archangels and angels adore Thee,
  Cherubim wonder, and seraphs admire;
Therefore we praise Thee, rejoicing before Thee,
  Joining in rapture the heavenly choir.

Glorious in holiness, fearful in praises,
  Who shall not fear Thee, and who shall not laud?
Anthems of glory Thy universe raises,
  Holy and Infinite! Father and God!

CALLED

Partakers of the heavenly calling.—Hebrews 3:1.

HOLY brethren, called and chosen by the sovereign Voice of Might,
See your high and holy calling out of darkness into light!
Called according to His purpose and the riches of His love;
Won to listen by the leading of the gentle heavenly Dove!

Called to suffer with our Master, patiently to run His race;
Called a blessing to inherit, called to holiness and grace;
Called to fellowship with Jesus, by the Ever-Faithful One;
Called to His eternal glory, to the kingdom of His Son.

Whom He calleth He preserveth, and His glory they shall see;
He is faithful that hath called you,—He will do it, fear not ye!
Therefore, holy brethren, onward! thus ye make your calling sure;
For the prize of this high calling, bravely to the end endure.

TRUSTING JESUS

I.

I AM trusting Thee, Lord Jesus,
    Trusting only Thee;
Trusting Thee for full salvation,
    Great and free.

II.

I am trusting Thee for pardon;
    At Thy feet I bow,
For Thy grace and tender mercy,
    Trusting now.

III.

I am trusting Thee for cleansing
    In the crimson flood;
Trusting Thee to make me holy
    By Thy blood.

IV.

I am trusting Thee to guide me;
    Thou alone shalt lead!
Every day and hour supplying
    All my need.

V.

I am trusting Thee for power;
    Thine can never fail!
Words which Thou Thyself shalt give me,
    Must prevail.

VI.

I am trusting Thee, Lord Jesus;
    Never let me fall!
I am trusting Thee for ever,
    And for all.

TO THEE

Lord, to whom shall we go?—John 6:68.

I BRING my sins to Thee,
   The sins I cannot count,
That all may cleansed be
   In Thy once opened Fount.
I bring them, Saviour, all to Thee,
The burden is too great for me.

My heart to Thee I bring,
   The heart I cannot read;
A faithless, wandering thing,
   An evil heart indeed.
I bring it, Saviour, now to Thee,
That fixed and faithful it may be.

To Thee I bring my care,
   The care I cannot flee;
Thou wilt not only share,
   But bear it all for me.
O loving Saviour, now to Thee
I bring the load that wearies me.

I bring my grief to Thee,
   The grief I cannot tell;
No words shall needed be,
   Thou knowest all so well.
I bring the sorrow laid on me,
O suffering Saviour, now to Thee.

My joys to Thee I bring,
   The joys Thy love hath given,
That each may be a wing
   To lift me nearer heaven.
I bring them, Saviour, all to Thee,
For Thou hast purchased all for me.

My life I bring to Thee,
   I would not be my own;
O Saviour, let me be
   Thine ever, Thine alone.
My heart, my life, my all I bring
To Thee, my Saviour and my King!

I COULD NOT DO WITHOUT THEE

I COULD not do without Thee,
  O Saviour of the lost!
Whose precious blood redeemed me,
  At such tremendous cost.
Thy righteousness, Thy pardon,
  Thy precious blood must be
My only hope and comfort,
  My glory and my plea!

I could not do without Thee!
  I cannot stand alone,
I have no strength or goodness,
  No wisdom of my own.
But Thou, beloved Saviour,
  Art all in all to me;
And weakness will be power,
  If leaning hard on Thee.

I could not do without Thee!
  For oh! the way is long,
And I am often weary,
  And sigh replaces song.
How *could* I do without Thee?
  I do not know the way;
Thou knowest and Thou leadest,
  And wilt not let me stray.

I could not do without Thee,
  O Jesus, Saviour dear!
E'en when my eyes are holden,
  I know that Thou art near.
How dreary and how lonely
  This changeful life would be,
Without the sweet communion,
  The secret rest with Thee!

I could not do without Thee!
  No other friend can read
The spirit's strange deep longings,
  Interpreting its need.

No human heart could enter
   Each dim recess of mine,
And soothe and hush and calm it,
   O blessed Lord, but Thine!

I could not do without Thee!
   For years are fleeting fast,
And soon, in solemn loneliness,
   The river must be passed.
But Thou wilt never leave me,
   And, though the waves roll high,
I know Thou wilt be near me,
And whisper, "It is I."

"I DID THIS FOR THEE! WHAT HAST THOU DONE FOR ME?"

(MOTTO PLACED UNDER A PICTURE OF OUR SAVIOUR
IN THE STUDY OF A GERMAN DIVINE.)

I GAVE My life for thee,	Galatians 2:20.
My precious blood I shed,	1 Peter 1:19
That thou might'st ransomed be,	Ephesians 1:7.
And quickened from the dead.	Ephesians 2:1
I gave My life for thee;	Titus 2:14
What hast thou given for Me?	John 21:15–17.
I spent long years for thee	1 Timothy 1:15.
In weariness and woe,	Isaiah 53:3.
That an eternity	John 17:24.
Of joy thou mightest know.	John 16:22.
I spent long years for thee;	John 1:10–11.
Hast thou spent *one* for Me?	1 Peter 4:2.
My Father's home of light,	John 17:5.
My rainbow-circled throne,	Revelation 4:3
I left, for earthly night,	Philippians 2:7.
For wanderings sad and lone.	Matthew 8:20.
I left it all for thee;	2 Corinthians 8:9.
Hast thou left aught for Me?	Luke 10:29.
I suffered much for thee,	Isaiah 53:5.
More than thy tongue may tell,	Matthew 26:39.
Of bitterest agony,	Luke 22:44.
To rescue thee from hell.	Romans 5:9.
I suffered much for thee;	1 Peter 2:21–24.
What canst thou bear for Me?	Romans 8:17–18.

And I have brought to thee,	John 4:10, 14.
Down from My home above,	John 3:13.
Salvation full and free,	Revelation 21:6.
My pardon and My love.	Acts 5:31.
Great gifts I brought to thee;	Psalm 68:18.
What hast thou brought to Me?	Romans 12:1.
Oh, let thy life be given,	Romans 6:13.
Thy years for Him be spent,	2 Corinthians 5:15.
World-fetters all be riven,	Philippians 3:8.
And joy with suffering blent;	1 Peter 4:13–16.
I gave Myself for thee:	Ephesians 5:2.
Give thou *thyself* to Me!	Proverbs 23:26.

IN FULL AND GLAD SURRENDER

"In full and glad surrender
We give ourselves to Thee,
Thine utterly, and only,
And evermore to be!

"O Son of God, who lovest us,
We will be Thine alone,
And all we are, and all we have,
Shall henceforth be Thine own!"

Reign over us, Lord Jesus;
O make our heart thy throne:
It shall be thine, dear Savior,
It shall be thine alone.

O come and reign, Lord Jesus;
Rule over everything!
And keep us always loyal,
And true to thee, our King.

EVENING TEARS AND MORNING SONGS

Weeping may endure in the evening,
but singing cometh in the morning,
                    —Psalm 30:5 (*Margin*).

In the evening there is weeping,
    Lengthening shadows, failing sight;
Silent darkness slowly creeping
    Over all things dear and bright.

In the evening there is weeping,
    Lasting all the twilight through;
Phantom shadows, never sleeping,
    Wakening slumbers of the true.

In the morning cometh singing,
    Cometh joy and cometh sight,
When the sun ariseth, bringing
    Healing on his wings of light.

In the morning cometh singing,
    Songs that ne'er in silence end,
Angel minstrels ever bringing
    Praises new with thine to blend.

Are the twilight shadows casting
    Heavy glooms upon thy heart?
Soon in radiance everlasting
    Night for ever shall depart.

Art thou weeping, sad and lonely,
    Through the evening of thy days?
All thy sighing shall be only
    Prelude of more perfect praise.

Darkest hour is nearest dawning,
    Solemn herald of the day;
Singing cometh in the morning,
    God shall wipe thy tears away!

INCREASE OUR FAITH

Lord, increase our faith.—Luke 17:5.

I.

INCREASE our faith, beloved Lord!
  For Thou alone canst give
The faith that takes Thee at Thy word,
  The faith by which we live.

II.

Increase our faith! So weak are we,
  That we both may and must
Commit our very faith to Thee,
  Entrust to Thee our trust.

III.

Increase our faith! for there is yet
  Much land to be possessed;
And by no other strength we get
  Our heritage of rest.

IV.

Increase our faith! On this broad shield
  "All" fiery darts be caught;
We must be victors in the field
  Where Thou for us hast fought.

V.

Increase our faith, that we may claim
  Each starry promise sure,
And *always* triumph in Thy name,
  And to the end endure.

VI.

Increase our faith, O Lord, we pray,
  That we may not depart
From Thy commands, but *all* obey
  With free and loyal heart.

VII.

Increase our faith—increase it still—
   From heavenward hour to hour,
And in us gloriously "fulfil
   The work of faith with power."

VIII.

Increase our faith, that never dim
   Or trembling it may be,
Crowned with the "perfect peace" of him
   "Whose mind is stayed on Thee."

IX.

Increase our faith, for Thou hast prayed
   That it should never fail;
Our stedfast anchorage is made
   With Thee, within the veil.

X.

Increase our faith, that unto Thee
   More fruit may still abound;
That it may grow "exceedingly,"
   And to Thy praise be found.

XI.

Increase our faith, O Saviour dear,
   By Thy sweet sovereign grace,
Till, changing faith for vision clear,
   We see Thee face to face!

IS IT FOR ME?

O Thou whom my soul loveth.
　　　—Song of Solomon 1:7.

Is it for me, dear Saviour,
　Thy glory and Thy rest?
For me, so weak and sinful,
　Oh, shall *I* thus be blessed?
Is it for me to see Thee
　In all Thy glorious grace,
And gaze in endless rapture
　On Thy beloved Face?

Is it for me to listen
　To Thy beloved Voice,
And hear its sweetest music
　Bid even me rejoice?
Is it for me, Thy welcome,
　Thy gracious "Enter in"?
For me, Thy "Come, ye blessed!"
　For me, so full of sin?

O Saviour, precious Saviour,
　My heart is at Thy feet;
I bless Thee and I love Thee,
　And Thee I long to meet.
A thrill of solemn gladness
　Has hushed my very heart,
To think that I shall really
　Behold Thee as Thou art;

Behold Thee in Thy beauty,
　Behold Thee face to face;
Behold Thee in Thy glory,
　And reap Thy smile of grace;
And be with Thee for ever,
　And never grieve Thee more!
Dear Saviour, I *must* praise Thee,
　And lovingly adore.

JUSTIFIED

This is the name wherewith she shall be called,
The Lord our Righteousness.—Jeremiah 33:16.

ISRAEL of God, awaken! Church of Christ, arise and shine
Mourning garb and soiled raiment henceforth be no longer thine!
For the Lord thy God hath clothed thee with a new and glorious dress,
With the garments of salvation, with the robe of righteousness.

By the grace of God the Father, thou art freely justified,
Through the great redemption purchased by the blood of Him who died;
By His life, for thee fulfilling God's command exceeding broad,
By His glorious resurrection, seal and signet of thy God.

Therefore, justified for ever by the faith which He hath given,
Peace, and joy, and hope abounding, smooth thy trial path to heaven:
Unto Him betrothed for ever, who thy life shall crown and bless,
By His name thou shalt be called, Christ, "The Lord our Righteousness!"

COVENANT BLESSINGS

He hath made with me an everlasting covenant,
ordered in all things, and sure.—2 Samuel 23:5.

JEHOVAH'S Covenant shall endure,
All ordered, everlasting, sure!
O child of God, rejoice to trace
Thy portion in its glorious grace.

'Tis thine, for Christ is given to be
The Covenant of God to thee:
In Him, God's golden scroll of light,
The darkest truths are clear and bright.

O sorrowing sinner, well He knew,
Ere time began, what He would do!
Then rest thy hope within the veil;
His covenant mercies shall not fail.

O doubting one, the Eternal Three
Are pledged in faithfulness for thee;
Claim every promise, sweet and sure,
By covenant oath of God secure.

O waiting one, each moment's fall
Is marked by love that planned them all;
Thy times, all ordered by His hand,
In God's eternal covenant stand.

O feeble one, look up and see
Strong consolation sworn for thee;
Jehovah's glorious arm is shown,
His covenant strength is all thine own.

O mourning one, each stroke of love
A covenant blessing yet shall prove;
His covenant love shall be thy stay;
His covenant grace be as thy day.

O Love that chose, O Love that died,
O Love that sealed and sanctified!
All glory, glory, glory be,
O covenant Triune God, to Thee!

NEW YEAR HYMN

JESUS, blessed Saviour,
  Help us now to raise
Songs of glad thanksgiving,
  Songs of holy praise.
O how kind and gracious
  Thou hast always been!
O how many blessings
  Every day has seen!
    Jesus, blessed Saviour,
      Now our praises hear,
      For Thy grace and favour
      Crowning all the year.

Jesus, holy Saviour,
  Only Thou canst tell
How we often stumbled,
  How we often fell!
All our sins (so many!),
  Saviour, Thou dost know;
In Thy blood most precious,
  Wash us white as snow.
    Jesus, blessed Saviour,
      Keep us in Thy fear,
      Let Thy grace and favour
      Pardon all the year.

Jesus, loving Saviour,
  Only Thou dost know
All that may befall us
  As we onward go.
So we humbly pray Thee,
  Take us by the hand,
Lead us ever upward
  To the Better Land.
    Jesus, blessed Saviour,
      Keep us ever near,
      Let Thy grace and favour
      Shield us all the year.

Jesus, precious Saviour,
  Make us all Thine own,
Make us Thine for ever,
  Make us Thine alone.
Let each day, each moment,
  Of this glad New-year,
Be for Jesus only,
  Jesus, Saviour dear.
    Then, O blessed Saviour,
      Never need we fear,
    For Thy grace and favour
      Crown our bright New-year!

WHOM I SERVE

Jesus, Master, whom I serve,
  Though so feebly and so ill,
Strengthen hand and heart and nerve
  All Thy bidding to fulfil;
Open Thou mine eyes to see
All the work Thou hast for me.

Lord, Thou needest not, I know,
  Service such as I can bring;
Yet I long to prove and show
  Full allegiance to my King.
Thou an honour[1] art to me,
Let me be a praise to Thee.

Jesus, Master! wilt Thou use
  One who owes Thee more than all?
As Thou wilt! I would not choose,
  Only let me hear Thy call.
Jesus! let me always be
In Thy service glad and free.

---

1 See marginal reading of 1 Peter 2:7.

WHOSE I AM

JESUS, Master, whose I am,
   Purchased Thine alone to be,
By Thy blood, O spotless Lamb,
   Shed so willingly for me;
Let my heart be all Thine own,
Let me live to Thee alone.

Other lords have long held sway;
   Now, Thy name alone to bear,
Thy dear voice alone obey,
   Is my daily, hourly prayer.
Whom have I in heaven but Thee?
Nothing else my joy can be.

Jesus, Master! I am Thine;
   Keep me faithful, keep me near;
Let Thy presence in me shine
   All my homeward way to cheer.
Jesus! at Thy feet I fall,
Oh, be Thou my All-in-all.

"JESUS ONLY"

And when they had lifted up their eyes,
they saw no man, save Jesus only.—Matthew 17:8.

I.

"JESUS only!" In the shadow
   Of the cloud so chill and dim,
We are clinging, loving, trusting,
   He with us, and we with Him;
All unseen, though ever nigh,
"Jesus only"—all our cry.

II.

"Jesus only!" In the glory,
   When the shadows all are flown,
Seeing Him in all His beauty,
   Satisfied with Him alone;
May we join His ransomed throng,
"Jesus only"—all our song!

JOINED TO CHRIST

Head over all things to the Church, which is His body.
—Ephesians 1:22–23.

JOINED to Christ in mystic union,
　　We Thy members, Thou our Head,
Sealed by deep and true communion,
　　Risen with Thee, who once were dead—
Saviour, we would humbly claim
All the power of this Thy name.

Instant sympathy to brighten
　　All their weakness and their woe,
Guiding grace their way to lighten,
　　Shall Thy loving members know;
All their sorrows Thou dost bear,
All Thy gladness they shall share.

Make Thy members every hour
　　For Thy blessed service meet;
Earnest tongues, and arms of power,
　　Skilful hands, and hastening feet,
Ever ready to fulfil
All Thy word and all Thy will.

Everlasting life Thou givest,
　　Everlasting love to see;
They shall live because Thou livest,
　　And their life is hid with Thee.
Safe Thy members shall be found,
When their glorious Head is crowned!

JUST WHEN THOU WILT[1]

I.
JUST when Thou wilt, O Master, call!
Or at the noon, or evening fall,
Or in the dark, or in the light,—
Just when Thou wilt, it must be right.

II.
Just when Thou wilt, O Saviour, come,
Take me to dwell in Thy bright home!
Or when the snows have crowned my head,
Or ere it hath one silver thread.

III.
Just when Thou wilt, O Bridegroom, say,
"Rise up, my love, and come away!"
Open to me Thy golden gate
Just when Thou wilt, or soon, or late.

IV.
Just when Thou wilt—Thy time is best—
Thou shalt appoint my hour of rest,
Marked by the Sun of perfect love,
Shining unchangeably above.

V.
Just when Thou wilt!—no choice for me!
Life is a gift to use for Thee;
Death is a hushed and glorious tryst,
With Thee, my King, my Saviour, Christ!

THE ETERNITY OF GOD

The King eternal, immortal, invisible.
—1 Timothy 1:17.

King Eternal and Immortal!
  We, the children of an hour,
Bend in lowly adoration,
Rise in raptured admiration,
    At the whisper of Thy power.
      Myriad ages in Thy sight
        Are but as the fleeting day;
      Like a vision of the night,
        Worlds may rise and pass away.

All Thy glories are eternal,
  None shall ever pass away;
Truth and mercy all victorious,
Righteousness and love all glorious,
    Shine with everlasting ray:
      All resplendent, ere the light
        Bade primeval darkness flee;
      All transcendent, through the flight
        Of eternities to be.

Thou art God from everlasting,
  And to everlasting art!
Ere the dawn of shadowy ages,
Dimly guessed by angel sages,
    Ere the beat of seraph-heart;
      Thou, Jehovah, art the same,
        And Thy years shall have no end
      Changeless nature, changeless name,
        Ever Father, God, and Friend!

LIGHT AFTER DARKNESS

Light after darkness,
  Gain after loss,
Strength after suffering,
  Crown after cross.
Sweet after bitter,
  Song after sigh,
Home after wandering,
  Praise after cry.

"Sheaves after sowing,
  Sun after rain,
Sight after mystery,
  Peace after pain.
Joy after sorrow,
  Calm after blast,
Rest after weariness,
  Sweet rest at last.

"Near after distant,
  Gleam after gloom,
Love after loneliness,
  Life after tomb.
After long agony,
  Rapture of bliss!
Right was the pathway
  Leading to this!"

PERFECT PEACE

IN ILLNESS

I.
LIKE a river glorious
　Is God's perfect peace,
Over all victorious
　In its bright increase.
Perfect—yet it floweth
　Fuller every day;
Perfect—yet it groweth
　Deeper all the way.

Chorus
Stayed upon Jehovah,
　Hearts are fully blest,
Finding, as He promised,
　Perfect peace and rest.

II.
Hidden in the hollow
　Of His blessed hand,
Never foe can follow,
　Never traitor stand.
Not a surge of worry,
　Not a shade of care,
Not a blast of hurry
　Touch the spirit there.

III.
Every joy or trial
　Falleth from above,
Traced upon our dial
　By the Sun of Love.
We may trust Him solely
　All for us to do;
They who trust Him wholly,
　Find Him wholly true.

A WORKER'S PRAYER

LORD, speak to me, that I may speak
  In living echoes of Thy tone;
As Thou hast sought, so let me seek
  Thy erring children, lost and lone.

O lead me, Lord, that I may lead
  The wandering and the wavering feet;
O feed me, Lord, that I may feed
  Thy hungering ones with manna sweet.

O strengthen me, that while I stand
  Firm on the Rock and strong in Thee,
I may stretch out a loving hand
  To wrestlers with the troubled sea.

O teach me, Lord, that I may teach
  The precious things Thou dost impart;
And wing my words, that they may reach
  The hidden depths of many a heart.

O give Thine own sweet rest to me,
  That I may speak with soothing power
A word in season, as from Thee,
  To weary ones in needful hour.

O fill me with Thy fulness, Lord,
  Until my very heart o'erflow
In kindling thought and glowing word,
  Thy love to tell, Thy praise to show.

O use me, Lord, use even me,
  Just *as* Thou wilt, and *when*, and *where;*
Until Thy blessed Face I see,
  Thy rest, Thy joy, Thy glory share.

"MASTER, SAY ON!"

Master, speak! Thy servant heareth,
  Waiting for Thy gracious word,
Longing for Thy voice that cheereth;
  Master! let it now be heard.
I am listening, Lord, for Thee;
What hast Thou to say to me?

Master, speak in love and power:
  Crown the mercies of the day,
In this quiet evening hour
  Of the moonrise o'er the bay,
With the music of Thy voice;
Speak! and bid Thy child rejoice.

Often through my heart is pealing
  Many another voice than Thine,
Many an unwilled echo stealing
  From the walls of this Thy shrine:
Let Thy longed-for accents fall;
Master, speak! and silence all.

Master, speak! I do not doubt Thee,
  Though so tearfully I plead;
Saviour, Shepherd! oh, without Thee
  Life would be a blank indeed!
But I long for fuller light,
Deeper love, and clearer sight.

Resting on the "faithful saying,"
  Trusting what Thy gospel saith,
On Thy written promise staying
  All my hope in life and death,
Yet I long for something more
From Thy love's exhaustless store.

Speak to me by name, O Master,
  Let me *know* it is to me;
Speak, that I may follow faster,
  With a step more firm and free,
Where the Shepherd leads the flock,
In the shadow of the Rock.

Master, speak! I kneel before Thee,
    Listening, longing, waking still;
Oh, how long shall I implore Thee
    This petition to fulfil!
Hast Thou not one word for me?
Must my prayer unanswered be?

Master, speak! Though least and lowest,
    Let me not unheard depart;
Master, speak! for oh, Thou knowest
    All the yearning of my heart,
Knowest all its truest need;
Speak! and make me blest indeed.

Master, speak! and make me ready,
    When Thy voice is truly heard,
With obedience glad and steady
    Still to follow every word.
I am listening, Lord, for Thee;
Master, speak, oh, speak to me!

A HAPPY NEW YEAR TO YOU

NEW mercies, new blessings, new light on thy way;
New courage, new hope, and new strength for each day;
New notes of thanksgiving, new chords of delight,
New praise in the morning, new songs in the night;
New wine in thy chalice, new altars to raise;
New fruits for thy Master, new garments of praise;
New gifts from His treasures, new smiles from His face;
New streams from the fountain of infinite grace;
New stars for thy crown, and new tokens of love;
New gleams of the glory that waits thee above;
New light of His countenance full and unpriced;—
All this be the joy of thy new life in Christ!

NOBODY KNOWS BUT JESUS

I.
"NOBODY knows but Jesus!"
　'Tis only the old refrain
Of a quaint, pathetic slave-song,
　But it comes again and again.

II.
I only heard it quoted,
　And I do not know the rest;
But the music of the message
　Was wonderfully blessed.

III.
For it fell upon my spirit
　Like sweetest twilight psalm,
When the breezy sunset waters
　Die into starry calm.

IV.
"Nobody knows but Jesus!"
　Is it not better so,
That no one else but Jesus,
　My own dear Lord, should know?

V.
When the sorrow is a secret
　Between my Lord and me,
I learn the fuller measure
　Of His quick sympathy.

VI.
Whether it be so heavy,
　That dear ones could not bear
To know the bitter burden
　They could not come and share:

VII.

Whether it be so tiny,
    That others could not see
Why it should be a trouble,
    And seem so real to me;

VIII.

Either and both, I lay them
    Down at my Master's feet,
And find them, alone with Jesus,
    Mysteriously sweet.

IX.

Sweet, for they bring me closer
    To the dearest, truest Friend;
Sweet, for He comes the nearer,
    As 'neath the cross I bend;

X.

Sweet, for they are the channels
    Through which His teachings flow;
Sweet, for by these dark secrets
    His heart of love I know.

XI.

"Nobody knows but Jesus!"
    It is music for to-day,
And through the darkest hours
    It will chime along the way.

XII.

"Nobody knows but Jesus!"
    My Lord, I bless Thee now,
For the sacred gift of sorrow
    That no one knows but Thou.

NOT YOUR OWN

"NOT your own!" but His ye are,
  Who hath paid a price untold
For your life, exceeding far
  All earth's store of gems and gold.
With the precious blood of Christ,
Ransom treasure all unpriced,
Full redemption is procured,
Full salvation is assured.

"Not your own!" but His by right,
  His peculiar treasure now,
Fair and precious in His sight,
  Purchased jewels for His brow.
He will keep what thus He sought,
Safely guard the dearly bought,
Cherish that which He did choose,
Always love and never lose.

"Not your own!" but His, the King,
  His, the Lord of earth and sky,
His, to whom archangels bring
  Homage deep and praises high.
What can royal birth bestow?
Or the proudest titles show?
Can such dignity be known
As the glorious name, "His own!"

"Not your own!" To Him ye owe
  All your life and all your love;
Live, that ye His praise may show,
  Who is yet all praise above.
Every day and every hour,
Every gift and every power,
Consecrate to Him alone,
Who hath claimed you for His own.

(Continued)

Teach us, Master, how to give
   All we have and are to Thee;
Grant us, Saviour, while we live,
   Wholly, only, Thine to be.
Henceforth be our calling high
Thee to serve and glorify;
Ours no longer, but Thine own,
Thine for ever, Thine alone!

NOTHING TO PAY

NOTHING to pay! Ah, nothing to pay!
Never a word of excuse to say!
Year after year thou hast filled the score,
Owing thy Lord still more and more.
 Hear the voice of Jesus say,
"Verily thou hast nothing to pay!
Ruined, lost art thou, and yet
I forgave thee all that debt."

Nothing to pay! the debt is so great;
What will you do with the awful weight?
How shall the way of escape be made?
Nothing to pay! yet it must be paid!
 Hear the voice of Jesus say,
"Verily thou hast nothing to pay!
All has been put to My account,
I have paid the full amount."

Nothing to pay; yes, nothing to pay!
Jesus has cleared all the debt away;
Blotted it out with His bleeding hand!
Free and forgiven and loved you stand.
 Hear the voice of Jesus say,
"Verily thou hast nothing to pay!
Paid is the debt, and the debtor free!
Now I ask *thee*, lovest thou ME?"

THE ANGELS' SONG

Now let us sing the Angels' Song,
  That rang so sweet and clear,
When heavenly light and music fell
  On earthly eye and ear,—
To Him we sing, our Saviour King,
  Who always deigns to hear:
    "Glory to God! and peace on earth."

He came to tell the Father's love,
  His goodness, truth, and grace;
To show the brightness of His smile,
  The glory of His face;
With His own light, so full and bright,
  The shades of death to chase.
    "Glory to God! and peace on earth."

He came to bring the weary ones
  True peace and perfect rest;
To take away the guilt and sin
  Which darkened and distressed;
That great and small might hear His call,
  And all in Him be blessed.
    "Glory to God! and peace on earth."

He came to bring a glorious gift,
  "Goodwill to men;"—and why?
Because He loved us, Jesus came
  For us to live and die.
Then, sweet and long, the Angels' Song
  Again we raise on high:
    "Glory to God! and peace on earth."

EVENING PRAYER

Now the light has gone away,
Saviour, listen while I pray,
Asking Thee to watch and keep,
And to send me quiet sleep.

Jesus, Saviour, wash away
All that has been wrong to-day,
Help me every day to be
Good and gentle, more like Thee.

Let my near and dear ones be
Always near and dear to Thee;
Oh, bring me and all I love
To Thy happy home above!

Now my evening praise I give:
Thou didst die that I might live,
All my blessings come from Thee;
Oh, how good Thou art to me!

Thou, my best and kindest Friend,
Thou wilt love me to the end!
Let me love Thee more and more.
Always better than before!

NOW AND AFTERWARD

Now, the sowing and the weeping,
  Working hard and waiting long;
Afterward, the golden reaping,
  Harvest home and grateful song.

Now, the pruning, sharp, unsparing;
  Scattered blossom, bleeding shoot!
Afterward, the plenteous bearing
  Of the Master's pleasant fruit.

Now, the plunge, the briny burden,
  Blind, faint gropings in the sea;
Afterward, the pearly guerdon
  That shall make the diver free.

Now, the long and toilsome duty
  Stone by stone to carve and bring;
Afterward, the perfect beauty
  Of the palace of the King.

Now, the tuning and the tension,
  Wailing minors, discord strong;
Afterward, the grand ascension
  Of the Alleluia song.

Now, the spirit conflict-riven,
  Wounded heart, unequal strife;
Afterward, the triumph given,
  And the victor's crown of life.

Now, the training, strange and lowly,
  Unexplained and tedious now;
Afterward, the service holy,
  And the Master's "Enter thou!"

THE ESSENTIAL BLESSEDNESS OF GOD

Dwelling in the light.—1 Timothy 6:16.

O GLORIOUS God and King,
  O gracious Father, hear
The praise our hearts would bring
  To Thee, who, ever near,
Yet in eternity dost dwell,
Immortal and invisible.

Around Thee all is light,
  And rest of perfect love,
And glory full and bright,
  All human thought above:
Thyself the Fountain infinite
Of all ineffable delight.

O depth of holy bliss,
  Essential and Divine!
What thought can measure this,—
  Thy joy, *Thy* glory,—Thine!
Yet such our treasure evermore,
Thy fulness is Thy children's store.

O Father, Thy great grace
  We magnify and praise;
Called to that blessed place,
  With Thee through endless days
Thy joy to share, Thy joy to be,
Thy glory all unveiled to see!

SUNDAY BELLS[1]

O SWEET Sabbath bells!
A message of musical chiming
Ye bring us from God, and we know what you say;
    Now rising, now falling,
    So tunefully calling
His children to seek Him, and praise Him to-day.

    The day we love best!
    The brightest and best of the seven,
The pearl of the week, and the light of our way;
    We hold it a treasure,
    And count it a pleasure,
To welcome its dawning and praise Him to-day.

    O sweet Sabbath rest!
    The gift of our Father in heaven;
A herald sent down from the home far away,
    With peace for the weary,
    And joy for the dreary:
Then, oh! let us thank Him, and praise Him to-day.

    Rejoice and be glad!
    'Tis the day of our Saviour and Brother,
The Life that is risen, the Truth and the Way;
    Salvation He brought us
    When wand'ring He sought us,
With blood He hath bought us: then praise Him to-day.

---

1 From "Sacred Songs for Little Singers," Novello & Co.

CHOSEN IN CHRIST

He hath chosen us in Him before the foundation of the world.
—Ephesians 1:4.

O THOU chosen Church of Jesus, glorious, blessed, and secure,
Founded on the One Foundation, which for ever shall endure;
Not thy holiness or beauty can thy strength and safety be,
But the everlasting love wherewith Jehovah loved thee.

Chosen—by His own good pleasure, by the counsel of His will,
Mystery of power and wisdom working for His people still;
Chosen—in thy mighty Saviour, ere one ray of quickening light
Beamed upon the chaos, waiting for the Word of sovereign might.

Chosen—through the Holy Spirit, through the sanctifying grace
Poured upon His precious vessels, meetened for the heavenly place;
Chosen—to show forth His praises, to be holy in His sight;
Chosen—unto grace and glory, chosen unto life and light.

Blessed be the God and Father of our Saviour Jesus Christ,
Who hath blessed us with such blessings all uncounted and unpriced!
Let our high and holy calling, and our strong salvation be,
Theme of never-ending praises, God of sovereign grace, to Thee!

EVERLASTING BLESSINGS

I know that whatsoever God doeth, it shall be for ever.
—Ecclesiastes 3:14.

Oh, what everlasting blessings God outpoureth on His own!
Ours by promise true and faithful, spoken from the eternal throne;
Ours by His eternal purpose ere the universe had place;
Ours by everlasting covenant, ours by free and royal grace.

With salvation everlasting He shall save us, He shall bless
With the largess of Messiah, everlasting righteousness;
Ours the everlasting mercy all His wondrous dealings prove;
Ours His everlasting kindness, fruit of everlasting love.

In the Lord Jehovah trusting, everlasting strength have we;
He Himself our Sun, our Glory, Everlasting Light shall be;
Everlasting life is ours, purchased by The Life laid down;
And our heads, oft bowed and weary, everlasting joy shall crown.

We shall dwell with Christ for ever, when the shadows flee away,
In the everlasting glory of the everlasting day.
Unto Thee, beloved Saviour, everlasting thanks belong,
Everlasting adoration, everlasting laud and song!

THINE IS THE POWER

Our Father, our Father, who dwellest in light,
We lean on Thy love, and we rest on Thy might;
In weakness and weariness joy shall abound,
For strength everlasting in Thee shall be found:
Our Refuge, our Helper in conflict and woe,
Our mighty Defender, how blessed to know
      That Thine is the Power!

Our Father, Thy promise we earnestly claim,
The sanctified heart that shall hallow Thy Name,
In ourselves, in our dear ones, throughout the wide world,
Be Thy Name as a banner of glory unfurled;
Let it triumph o'er evil and darkness and guilt,
We know Thou canst do it, we know that Thou wilt,
      For Thine is the Power!

Our Father, we long for the glorious day
When all shall adore Thee, and all shall obey.
Oh hasten Thy kingdom, oh show forth Thy might,
And wave o'er the nations Thy sceptre of right.
Oh make up Thy jewels, the crown of Thy love,
And reign in our hearts as Thou reignest above,
      For Thine is the Power!

Our Father, we pray that Thy will may be done,
For full acquiescence is heaven begun;—
Both in us and by us Thy purpose be wrought,
In word and in action, in spirit and thought;
And Thou canst enable us thus to fulfil,
With holy rejoicing, Thy glorious will,
      For Thine is the Power!

Our Father, Thou carest; Thou knowest indeed
Our inmost desires, our manifold need;
The fount of Thy mercies shall never be dry,
For Thy riches in glory shall mete the supply;
Our bread shall be given, our water be sure,
And nothing shall fail, for Thy word shall endure,
      And Thine is the Power!

Our Father, forgive us, for we have transgressed,
Have wounded Thy love, and forsaken Thy breast;
In the peace of Thy pardon henceforth let us live,
That through Thy forgiveness we too may forgive;
The Son of Thy love, who hath taught us to pray,
For Thy treasures of mercy hath opened the way,
       And Thine is the Power!

Thou knowest our dangers, Thou knowest our frame,
But a tower of strength is Thy glorious name;
Oh, lead us not into temptation, we pray,
But keep us, and let us not stumble or stray;
Thy children shall under Thy shadow abide;
In Thee as our Guide and our Shield we confide,
       For Thine is the Power!

Our Father, deliver Thy children from sin,
From evil without and from evil within,
From this world, with its manifold evil and wrong,
From the wiles of the Evil One, subtle and strong;
Till, as Christ overcame, we, too, conquer and sing,
All glory to Thee, our victorious King,
       For Thine is the Power!

Our Father, Thy children rejoice in Thy reign,
Rejoice in Thy highness, and praise Thee again!
Yea, Thine is the kingdom and Thine is the might,
And Thine is the glory transcendently bright;
For ever and ever that glory shall shine,
For ever and ever that kingdom be Thine,
       For Thine is the Power!

PRESENTED FAULTLESS

Behold I and the children which God hath given Me.
—Hebrews 2:13.

Our Saviour and our King,
Enthroned and crowned above,
Shall with exceeding gladness bring
The children of His love.

All that the Father gave
His glory shall behold;
Not one whom Jesus came to save
Is missing from His fold.

He shall confess His own
From every clime and coast,
Before His Father's glorious throne,
Before the angel host.

"O righteous Father, see,
In spotless robes arrayed,
Thy chosen gifts of love to Me,
Before the worlds were made.

"By new creation Thine;
By purpose and by grace,
By right of full redemption Mine,
Faultless before Thy face.

"As Thou hast loved Me,
So hast Thou loved them;
Thy precious jewels they shall be,
My glorious diadem!"

DISAPPOINTMENT

Our yet unfinished story
   Is tending all to this:
To God the greatest glory,
   To us the greatest bliss.

If all things work together
   For ends so grand and blest,
What need to wonder whether
   Each in itself is best!

If some things were omitted
   Or altered as we would,
The whole might be unfitted
   To work for perfect good.

Our plans may be disjointed,
   But we may calmly rest;
What God has once appointed
   Is better than our best.

We cannot see before us,
   But our all-seeing Friend
Is always watching o'er us,
   And knows the very end.

What though we seem to stumble?
   He will not let us fall;
And learning to be humble
   Is not lost time at all.

What though we fondly reckoned
   A smoother way to go
Than where His hand has beckoned?
   It will be better so.

What only seemed a barrier
   A stepping-stone shall be;
Our God is no long tarrier,
   A present help is He.

And when amid our blindness
   His disappointments fall,
We trust His loving-kindness
   Whose wisdom sends them all.

They are the purple fringes
   That hide His glorious feet;
They are the fire-wrought hinges
   Where truth and mercy meet;

By them the golden portal
   Of Providence shall ope,
And lift to praise immortal
   The songs of faith and hope.

From broken alabaster
   Was deathless fragrance shed,
The spikenard flowed the faster
   Upon the Saviour's head.

No shattered box of ointment
   We ever need regret,
For out of disappointment
   Flow sweetest odours yet.

The discord that involveth
   Some startling change of key,
The Master's hand resolveth
   In richest harmony.

We hush our children's laughter,
   When sunset hues grow pale;
Then, in the silence after,
   They hear the nightingale.

We mourned the lamp declining,
   That glimmered at our side;—
The glorious starlight shining
   Has proved a surer guide.

Then tremble not and shrink not

When Disappointment nears;
Be trustful still, and think not
   To realize all fears.

While we are meekly kneeling,
   We shall behold her rise,
Our Father's love revealing,
   An angel in disguise.

THE PRECIOUS BLOOD OF JESUS

I.

Precious, precious blood of Jesus,
    Shed on Calvary;
Shed for rebels, shed for sinners,
    Shed for me.

II.

Precious blood, that hath redeemed us!
    All the price is paid;
Perfect pardon now is offered,
    Peace is made.

III.

Precious, precious blood of Jesus,
    Let it make thee whole;
Let it flow in mighty cleansing
    O'er thy soul.

IV.

Though thy sins are red like crimson,
    Deep in scarlet glow,
Jesu's precious blood can make them
    White as snow.

V.

Now the holiest with boldness
    We may enter in,
For the open fountain cleanseth
    From all sin.

VI.

Precious blood! by this we conquer
    In the fiercest fight,
Sin and Satan overcoming
    By its might.

VII.

Precious, precious blood of Jesus,

Ever flowing free!
O believe it, O receive it,
    'Tis for thee!

VIII.
Precious blood, whose full atonement
    Makes us nigh to God!
Precious blood, our song of glory,
    Praise and laud!

RESTING

This is the rest wherewith ye may cause the weary to rest; and this is the refreshing.—Isaiah 28:12.

I.

RESTING on the faithfulness of Christ our Lord;
Resting on the fulness of His own sure word;
Resting on His power, on His love untold;
Resting on His covenant secured of old.

II.

Resting 'neath His guiding hand for untracked days;
Resting 'neath His shadow from the noontide rays;
Resting at the eventide beneath His wing,
In the fair pavilion of our Saviour King.

III.

Resting in the fortress while the foe is nigh;
Resting in the lifeboat while the waves roll high;
Resting in His chariot for the swift glad race;
Resting, always resting in His boundless grace.

IV.

Resting in the pastures, and beneath the Rock;
Resting by the waters where He leads His flock;
Resting, while we listen, at His glorious feet;
Resting in His very arms!—O rest complete!

V.

Resting and believing, let us onward press,
Resting in Himself, the Lord our Righteousness;
Resting and rejoicing, let His saved ones sing,
Glory, glory, glory be to Christ our King!

TRUST

SADLY bend the flowers
In the heavy rain;
After beating showers,
Sunbeams come again.
Little birds are silent
All the dark night through;
When the morning dawneth,
Their songs are sweet and new.

When a sudden sorrow
Comes like cloud and night,
Wait for God's to-morrow;
All will then be bright.
Only wait and trust Him
Just a little while;
After evening tear-drops
Shall come the morning smile.

OUR KING

Worship thou Him.—Psalm 45:11.

O Saviour, precious Saviour,
  Whom yet unseen we love;
O Name of might and favour,
  All other names above!
    We worship Thee, we bless Thee,
      To Thee alone we sing;
    We praise Thee, and confess Thee
      Our holy Lord and King!

O Bringer of salvation,
  Who wondrously hast wrought,
Thyself the revelation
  Of love beyond our thought!
    We worship Thee, we bless Thee,
      To Thee alone we sing;
    We praise Thee, and confess Thee
      Our gracious Lord and King!

In Thee all fulness dwelleth,
  All grace and power divine;
The glory that excelleth,
  O Son of God, is Thine:
    We worship Thee, we bless Thee,
      To Thee alone we sing;
    We praise Thee, and confess Thee
      Our glorious Lord and King!

Oh, grant the consummation
  Of this our song above,
In endless adoration,
  And everlasting love:
    Then shall we praise and bless Thee,
      Where perfect praises ring,
    And evermore confess Thee
      Our Saviour and our King!

HE HATH DONE IT!

I have blotted out, as a thick cloud, thy transgressions, and,
as a cloud, thy sins: return unto Me; for I have redeemed thee.
Sing, O ye heavens; for the Lord hath done it.—Isaiah 44:22–23.

I know that, whatsoever God doeth, it shall be for ever: nothing
can be put to it, nor anything taken from it.—Ecclesiastes 3:14.

Sing, O heavens! the Lord hath done it!
　Sound it forth o'er land and sea!
Jesus says, "I have redeemed thee,
　Now return, return to Me."
Oh return, for His own life-blood
　Paid the ransom, made us free
　　Evermore and evermore.

For I know that what He doeth
　Stands for ever, fixed and true;
Nothing can be added to it,
　Nothing left for us to do;
Nothing can be taken from it,
　Done for me and done for you,
　　Evermore and evermore.

Listen now! the Lord hath done it!
　For He loved us unto death;
It is finished! He has saved us!
　Only trust to what He saith.
He hath done it! Come and bless Him,
　Spend in praise your ransomed breath
　　Evermore and evermore.

O believe the Lord hath done it!
　Wherefore linger? wherefore doubt?
All the cloud of black transgression
　He Himself hath blotted out.
He hath done it! Come and bless Him,
　Swell the grand thanksgiving shout
　　Evermore and evermore.

SINGING FOR JESUS

With my song will I praise Him.—Psalm 28:7.

Sɪɴɢɪɴɢ for Jesus, our Saviour and King,
   Singing for Jesus, the Lord whom we love;
All adoration we joyously bring,
   Longing to praise as we praise Him above.

Singing for Jesus, our Master and Friend,
   Telling His love and His marvellous grace,
Love from eternity, love without end,
   Love for the loveless, the sinful and base.

Singing for Jesus, and trying to win
   Many to love Him, and join in the song;
Calling the weary and wandering in,
   Rolling the chorus of gladness along.

Singing for Jesus, our Life and our Light;
   Singing for Him as we press to the mark;
Singing for Him when the morning is bright,
   Singing, still singing, for Him in the dark.

Singing for Jesus, our Shepherd and Guide,
   Singing for gladness of heart that He gives;
Singing for wonder and praise that He died,
   Singing for blessing and joy that He lives.

Singing for Jesus, oh, singing with joy!
   Thus will we praise Him and tell out His love,
Till He shall call us to brighter employ,
   Singing for Jesus for ever above.

UNDER HIS SHADOW

(COMMUNION HYMN)

I sat down under His shadow with great delight.—Song of Solomon 2:3.

SIT down beneath His shadow,
  And rest with great delight;
The faith that now beholds Him
  Is pledge of future sight.

Our Master's love remember,
  Exceeding great and free;
Lift up thy heart in gladness,
  For He remembers thee.

Bring every weary burden,
  Thy sin, thy fear, thy grief;
He calls the heavy laden,
  And gives them kind relief.

His righteousness "all glorious"
  Thy festal robe shall be;
And love that passeth knowledge
  His banner over thee.

A little while, though parted,
  Remember, wait, and love,
Until He comes in glory,
  Until we meet above;

Till in the Father's kingdom
  The heavenly feast is spread,
And we behold His beauty,
  Whose blood for us was shed!

GLORIFIED

The God of all grace, who hath called you unto His eternal glory by Christ Jesus, . . . to Him be glory.—1 Peter 5:10–11.

SOVEREIGN Lord and gracious Master,
　Thou didst freely choose Thine own,
Thou hast called with mighty calling,
Thou wilt save, and keep from falling;
　Thine the glory, Thine alone!
　　Yet Thy hand shall crown in heaven
　　All the grace Thy love hath given;
　　Just, though undeserved, reward
　　From our glorious, gracious Lord.

From the martyr and apostle
　To the sainted baby boy,
Every consecrated chalice
In the King of Glory's palace
　Overflows with holy joy.
　　Sovereign choice of gift and dower,
　　Differing honour, differing power,—
　　Yet are all alike in this,
　　Perfect love and perfect bliss.

In those heavenly constellations,
　Lo! what differing glories meet;
Stars of radiance soft and tender,
Stars of full and dazzling splendour,
　All in God's own light complete;
　　Brightest they whose holy feet,
　　Faithful to His service sweet,
　　Nearest to their Master trod,
　　Winning wandering souls to God.

Oh the rapture of that vision!
　(Every earthly passion o'er),
Our Redeemer's coronation,
And the blissful exaltation
　Of the dear ones gone before.
　　Grace that shone for Christ below
　　Changed to glory we shall know;
　　And before His unveiled face
　　Sing the glory of His grace.

FAITHFUL PROMISES

Fear thou not; for I am with thee: be not dismayed; for I am thy God: I will strengthen thee; yea, I will help thee; yea, I will uphold thee with the right hand of my righteousness.—Isaiah 41:10.

NEW YEAR'S HYMN

STANDING at the portal
  Of the opening year,
Words of comfort meet us,
  Hushing every fear;
Spoken through the silence
  By our Father's voice,
Tender, strong, and faithful,
  Making us rejoice.
Onward then, and fear not,
  Children of the day!
For His word shall never,
  Never pass away!

I, the Lord, am with thee,
  Be thou not afraid!
I will help and strengthen,
  Be thou not dismayed!
Yea, I will uphold thee
  With my own right hand;
Thou art called and chosen
  In my sight to stand.
Onward then, and fear not,
  Children of the day!
For His word shall never,
  Never pass away!

For the year before us,
  Oh, what rich supplies!
For the poor and needy
  Living streams shall rise;
For the sad and sinful
  Shall His grace abound;
For the faint and feeble
  Perfect strength be found.

Onward then, and fear not,
   Children of the day!
For His word shall never,
   Never pass away!

He will never fail us,
   He will not forsake;
His eternal covenant
   He will never break!
Resting on His promise,
   What have we to fear?
God is all-sufficient
   For the coming year.
Onward then, and fear not,
   Children of the day!
For His word shall never,
   Never pass away!

CONSECRATION HYMN

Here we offer and present unto Thee, O Lord, ourselves, our souls and bodies, to be a reasonable, holy, and lively sacrifice unto Thee.

TAKE my life, and let it be
Consecrated, Lord, to Thee.

Take my moments and my days;
Let them flow in ceaseless praise.

Take my hands, and let them move
At the impulse of Thy love.

Take my feet, and let them be
Swift and "beautiful" for Thee.

Take my voice, and let me sing
Always, only, for my King.

Take my lips, and let them be
Filled with messages from Thee.

Take my silver and my gold;
Not a mite would I withhold.

Take my intellect, and use
Every power as Thou shalt choose.

Take my will, and make it Thine;
It shall be no longer mine.

Take my heart, it *is* Thine own;
It shall be Thy royal throne.

Take my love; my Lord, I pour
At Thy feet its treasure-store.

Take myself, and I will be
Ever, *only*, ALL for Thee.

TELL IT OUT

Tell it out among the heathen that the Lord is King.—Psalm 96:10.
(Prayer-Book Version)

TELL it out among the heathen that the Lord is King!
      Tell it out, tell it out!
Tell it out among the nations, bid them shout and sing!
      Tell it out, tell it out!
Tell it out with adoration, that He shall increase;
That the mighty King of Glory is the King of Peace.
Tell it out with jubilation, though the waves may roar,
That He sitteth on the water-floods, our King for evermore!
      Tell it out, etc.

Tell it out among the nations that the Saviour reigns!
      Tell it out, tell it out!
Tell it out among the heathen, bid them burst their chains!
      Tell it out, tell it out!
Tell it out among the weeping ones that Jesus lives;
Tell it out among the weary ones what rest He gives;
Tell it out among the sinners that He came to save;
Tell it out among the dying that He triumphed o'er the grave.
      Tell it out, etc.

Tell it out among the heathen Jesus reigns above!
      Tell it out, tell it out!
Tell it out among the nations that His name is Love!
      Tell it out, tell it out!
Tell it out among the highways, and the lanes at home;
Let it ring across the mountains and the ocean foam;
Like the sound of many waters let our glad shout be,
Till it echo and re-echo from the islands of the sea!
      Tell it out, etc.

ADVENT SONG

Thou art coming, O my Saviour!
  Thou art coming, O my King!
In Thy beauty all-resplendent,
In Thy glory all-transcendent;
  Well may we rejoice and sing!
Coming! in the opening east,
  Herald brightness slowly swells;
Coming! O my glorious Priest,
  Hear we not Thy golden bells?

Thou art coming, Thou art coming!
  We shall meet Thee on Thy way,
We shall see Thee, we shall know Thee,
We shall bless Thee, we shall show Thee
  All our hearts could never say!
What an anthem that will be,
Ringing out our love to Thee,
Pouring out our rapture sweet
At Thine own all-glorious feet!

Thou art coming! Rays of glory,
  Through the veil Thy death has rent,
Touch the mountain and the river
With a golden glowing quiver,
  Thrill of light and music blent.
Earth is brightened when this gleam
Falls on flower and rock and stream;
Life is brightened when this ray
Falls upon its darkest day.

Not a cloud and not a shadow,
  Not a mist and not a tear,
Not a sin and not a sorrow,
Not a dim and veiled to-morrow,
  For that sunrise grand and clear!
Jesus, Saviour, once with Thee,
  Nothing else seems worth a thought!
Oh, how marvellous will be
  All the bliss Thy pain hath bought!

Thou art coming! At Thy table
  We are witnesses for this,
While remembering hearts Thou meetest,
In communion clearest, sweetest,
  Earnest of our coming bliss.
Showing not Thy death alone,
  And Thy love exceeding great,
But Thy coming and Thy throne,
  All for which we long and wait.

Thou art coming! We are waiting
  With a hope that cannot fail;
Asking not the day or hour,
Resting on Thy word of power
  Anchored safe within the veil.
Time appointed may be long,
  But the vision must be sure:
Certainty shall make us strong,
  Joyful patience can endure!

Oh, the joy to see Thee reigning,
  Thee, my own beloved Lord!
Every tongue Thy name confessing,
Worship, honour, glory, blessing,
  Brought to Thee with glad accord!
Thee, my Master and my Friend,
  Vindicated and enthroned!
Unto earth's remotest end
  Glorified, adored, and owned!

THE FAITHFUL COMFORTER

The Holy Ghost—He is faithful.—Hebrews 10:15, 23.

To Thee, O Comforter Divine,
For all Thy grace and power benign,
    Sing we Alleluia!

To Thee, whose faithful love had place
In God's great Covenant of Grace,
    Sing we Alleluia!

To Thee, whose faithful voice doth win
The wandering from the ways of sin,
    Sing we Alleluia!

To Thee, whose faithful power doth heal,
Enlighten, sanctify, and seal,
    Sing we Alleluia!

To Thee, whose faithful truth is shown,
By every promise made our own,
    Sing we Alleluia!

To Thee, our Teacher and our Friend,
Our faithful Leader to the end,
    Sing we Alleluia!

To Thee, by Jesus Christ sent down,
Of all His gifts the sum and crown,
    Sing we Alleluia!

To Thee, who art with God the Son
And God the Father ever One,
    Sing we Alleluia! Amen!

TRUE-HEARTED, WHOLE-HEARTED

I.

TRUE-HEARTED, whole-hearted, faithful and loyal,
  King of our lives, by Thy grace we will be
Under Thy standard, exalted and royal,
  Strong in Thy strength, we will battle for Thee!

II.

True-hearted, whole-hearted! Fullest allegiance
  Yielding henceforth to our glorious King;
Valiant endeavour and loving obedience
  Freely and joyously now would we bring.

III.

True-hearted! Saviour, Thou knowest our story;
  Weak are the hearts that we lay at Thy feet,
Sinful and treacherous! yet, for Thy glory,
  Heal them, and cleanse them from sin and deceit.

IV.

Whole-hearted! Saviour, beloved and glorious,
  Take Thy great power, and reign Thou alone,
Over our wills and affections victorious,
  Freely surrendered, and wholly Thine own.

V.

Half-hearted, *false*-hearted! Heed we the warning!
  Only the whole can be perfectly true;
Bring the whole offering, all timid thought scorning,
  True-hearted only if whole-hearted too.

VI.

Half-hearted! Saviour, shall aught be withholden,
  Giving Thee part who hast given us all?
Blessings outpouring, and promises golden
  Pledging, with never reserve or recall.

VII.

Half-hearted! Master, shall any who know Thee
  Grudge Thee their lives, who hast laid down Thine own?
Nay; we would offer the hearts that we owe Thee,—
  Live for Thy love and Thy glory alone.

VIII.

Sisters, dear sisters, the call is resounding,
    Will ye not echo the silver refrain,
Mighty and sweet, and in gladness abounding,—
    "True-hearted, whole-hearted!" ringing again?

IX.

Jesus is with us, His rest is before us,
    Brightly His standard is waving above.
Brothers, dear brothers, in gathering chorus,
    Peal out the watchword of courage and love!

X.

Peal out the watchword, and silence it never,
    Song of our spirits, rejoicing and free!
"True-hearted, whole-hearted, now and for ever,
    King of our lives, by Thy grace we will be!"

THE SPIRITUALITY OF GOD

God is a Spirit.—John 4:24.

WHAT know we, Holy God, of Thee,
  Thy being and Thine essence pure?
Too bright the very mystery
  For mortal vision to endure.

We only know Thy word sublime,
  Thou art a Spirit! Perfect! One!
Unlimited by space or time,
  Unknown but through the eternal Son.

By change untouched, by thought untraced,
  And by created eye unseen,
In *Thy great Present* is embraced
  All that shall be, all that hath been.

O Father of our spirits, now
  We seek Thee in our Saviour's face;
In truth and spirit we would bow,
  And worship where we cannot trace.

ON THE LORD'S SIDE

Thine are we, David, and on thy side, thou son of Jesse.
—1 Chronicles 12:18.

I.

WHO is on the Lord's side?
  Who will serve the King?
Who will be His helpers,
  Other lives to bring?
Who will leave the world's side?
  Who will face the foe?
Who is on the Lord's side?
  Who for Him will go?
Response. By Thy call of mercy,
          By Thy grace divine,
      We are on the Lord's side;
        Saviour, we are Thine.

II.

Not for weight of glory,
  Not for crown and palm,
Enter we the army,
  Raise the warrior-psalm;
But for Love that claimeth
  Lives for whom He died:
He whom Jesus nameth
  Must be on His side.
Response. By Thy love constraining,
          By Thy grace divine,
      We are on the Lord's side;
        Saviour, we are Thine.

III.

Jesus, Thou hast bought us,
  Not with gold or gem,
But with Thine own life-blood,
  For Thy diadem.
With Thy blessing filling
  Each who comes to Thee,

Thou hast made us willing,
  Thou hast made us free.
Response. By Thy grand redemption,
    By Thy grace divine,
    We are on the Lord's side;
    Saviour, we are Thine.

IV.

Fierce may be the conflict,
  Strong may be the foe,
But the King's own army
  None can overthrow.
Round His standard ranging,
  Victory is secure,
For His truth unchanging
  Makes the triumph sure.
Response. Joyfully enlisting
    By Thy grace divine,
    We are on the Lord's side;
    Saviour, we are Thine.

V.

Chosen to be soldiers
  In an alien land;
"Chosen, called, and faithful,"
  For our Captain's band;
In the service royal
  Let us not grow cold;
Let us be right loyal,
  Noble, true, and bold.
Response. Master, Thou wilt keep us,
    By Thy grace divine,
    Always on the Lord's side,
    Saviour, always Thine!

WILL YOU NOT COME?

WILL you not come to Him for *Life?*
  Why will ye die, oh, why?
He gave His life for you, for you!
The gift is free, the word is true!
  Will you not come? oh, why will you die?

Will you not come to Him for *Peace?*
  Peace through His cross alone!
He shed His precious blood for you;
The gift is free, the word is true!
  He is our Peace—oh, is He your own?

Will you not come to Him for *Rest?*
  All that are weary, come!
The rest He gives is deep and true,
'Tis offered now, 'tis offered you!
  Rest in His love and rest in His home.

Will you not come to Him for *Joy?*
  Will you not come for this?
He laid His joys aside for you,
To give you joy so sweet, so true:
  Sorrowing heart, oh, drink of the bliss!

Will you not come to Him for *Love,*
  Love that can fill the heart?
Exceeding great, exceeding free!
He loveth you, He loveth me!
  Will you not come? Why stand you apart?

Will you not come to Him for ALL?
  Will you not "taste and see?"
He waits to give it all to you,
The gifts are free, the words are true!
  Jesus is calling, "Come unto Me!"

THY WILL BE DONE

Understanding what the will of the Lord is.—Ephesians 5:17.

WITH quivering heart and trembling will
   The word hath passed thy lips,
Within the shadow, cold and still,
   Of some fair joy's eclipse.
"Thy will be done!" Thy God hath heard,
And He will crown that faith-framed word.

Thy prayer shall be fulfilled: but how?
   His thoughts are not as thine;
While thou wouldst only weep and bow,
   He saith, "Arise and shine!"
Thy thoughts were all of grief and night,
But His of boundless joy and light.

Thy Father reigns supreme above:
   The glory of His name
Is Grace and Wisdom, Truth and Love,
   His will must be the same.
And thou hast asked all joys in one,
In whispering forth, "Thy will be done."

His will—each soul to sanctify
   Redeeming might hath won;[1]
His will—that thou shouldst never die,
   Believing on His Son;[2]
His will—that thou, through earthly strife,
Shouldst rise to everlasting life.[3]

That one unchanging song of praise
   Should from our hearts arise;[4]
That we should know His wondrous ways,
   Though hidden from the wise;[5]
That we, so sinful and so base,
Should know the glory of His grace.[6]

1 1 Thessalonians 4:3.
2 John 6:40.
3 John 6:39.
4 1 Thessalonians 5:18.
5 Matthew 11:25–26.
6 Ephesians 1:5–6, 11–12.

His will—to grant the yearning prayer
    For dear ones far away,[1]
That they His grace and love may share,
    And tread His pleasant way;
That in the Father and the Son
All perfect we may be in one.[2]

His will—the little flock to bring
    Into His royal fold,
To reign for ever with their King,[3]
    His beauty to behold.[4]
Sin's fell dominion crushed for aye,
Sorrow and sighing fled away.

This thou hast asked! And shall the prayer
    Float upward on a sigh?
No song were sweet enough to bear
    Such glad desires on high!
But God thy Father shall fulfil,
In thee and for thee, all His will.

---

1 1 John 5:14–16.
2 John 17:23–24.
3 Luke 12:32.
4 Isaiah 33:17.

WORTHY OF ALL ADORATION

"Worthy of all adoration,
  Is the Lamb that once was slain,"
Cry, in raptured exultation,
His redeemed from every nation;
  Angel myriads join the strain,
Sounding from their sinless strings
Glory to the King of kings:
Harping, with their harps of gold,
Praise which never can be told.

Hallelujahs full and swelling
  Rise around His throne of might,
All our highest laud excelling,
Holy and Immortal, dwelling
  In the unapproached light,
He is worthy to receive
All that heaven and earth can give;
Blessing, honour, glory, might,
All are His by glorious right.

As the sound of many waters
  Let the full Amen arise!
Hallelujah! Ceasing never,
Sounding through the great FOR EVER,
  Linking all its harmonies;
Through eternities of bliss,
Lord, our rapture shall be this;
And our endless life shall be
One AMEN of praise to Thee.

OUR COMMISSION

And the Spirit and the Bride say, Come. And let him that heareth say, Come.—Revelation 22:17.

Ye who hear the blessed call
    Of the Spirit and the Bride,
Hear the Master's word to all,
    Your commission and your guide—
"And let him that heareth say,
Come," to all yet far away.

"Come!" alike to age and youth;
    Tell them of our Friend above,
Of His beauty and His truth,
    Preciousness and grace and love;
Tell them what you know is true,
Tell them what He is to you.

"Come!" to those who never heard
    Why the Saviour's blood was shed;
Bear to them the message-word
    That can quicken from the dead;
Tell them Jesus "died for all,"
Tell them of His loving call.

"Come!" to those who do not care
    For the Saviour's precious death,
Having not a thought to spare
    For the gracious words He saith:
Ere the shadows gather deep,
Rouse them from their fatal sleep.

"Come!" to those who, while they hear,
    Linger, hardly knowing why;
Tell them that the Lord is near,
    Tell them Jesus passes by.
Call them *now*; oh, do not wait,
Lest to-morrow be too late!

"Come!" to those who wander far,
    Seeking, never finding, rest;
Point them to the Morning Star;

Show them how they may be blest
With the love that cannot cease,
Joyful hope and perfect peace.

"Come!" to those who draw in vain
    From the broken cisterns here,
Drinking but to thirst again;
    Tell them of the fountain near.
Living water, flowing still,
Free for "whosoever will."

"Come!" to those who faint and groan
    Under some unuttered grief,
Hearts that suffer all alone;
    Try to bring them true relief.
Tell them "Jesus wept," and He
Still is full of sympathy.

"Come!" to those who feel their sin,
    Fearing to be lost at last,
Mourning for the plague within,
    Mourning for transgressions past;
Tell them Jesus calls them in,
Heavy laden with their sin.

Such as these are all around,
    Meeting, passing, every day;
Ye who know the joyful sound,
    Have ye not a word to say?
Ye who hear that blessed "Come,"
Sweet and clear, can ye be dumb?

Brothers, sisters, do not wait,
    Speak for Him who speaks to you!
Wherefore should you hesitate?
    This is no great thing to do.
Jesus only bids you say,
"Come!" and will you not obey?

Lord! to Thy command we bow,
    Touch our lips with altar fire;
Let Thy Spirit kindle now
    Faith and zeal, and strong desire;
So that henceforth we may be
Fellow-workers, Lord, with Thee.

BE NOT WEARY

Yᴇs! He knows the way is dreary,
   Knows the weakness of our frame,
Knows that hand and heart are weary;
   He, "in all points," felt the same.
He is near to help and bless;
Be not weary, onward press.

Look to Him who once was willing
   All His glory to resign,
That, for thee the law fulfilling,
   All His merit might be thine.
Strive to follow day by day
Where His footsteps mark the way.

Look to Him, the Lord of Glory,
   Tasting death to win thy life;
Gazing on "that wondrous story,"
   Canst thou falter in the strife?
Is it not new life to know
That the Lord hath loved thee so?

Look to Him who ever liveth,
   Interceding for His own:
Seek, yea, claim the grace He giveth
   Freely from His priestly throne.
Will He not thy strength renew
With His Spirit's quickening dew?

Look to Him, and faith shall brighten,
   Hope shall soar, and love shall burn;
Peace once more thy heart shall lighten
   Rise! He calleth thee, return!
Be not weary on thy way,
Jesus is thy strength and stay.

A SILENCE AND A SONG

I AM alone, dear Master—
   Alone in heart with Thee!
Though merry faces round me
   And loving looks I see.

There's a hush among the blithe ones,
   While a pleasant voice is heard,
A truce to all the tournament
   Of flashing wit and word.

And in that truce of silence,
   I lay aside my lance,
And through the light and music send
   One happy upward glance.

I know not what the song may be,
   The words I cannot hear;
'Tis but a gentle melody,
   All simple, soft, and clear.

But the sweetness and the quiet
   Have set my spirit free,
And I turn in loving gladness,
   Dear Master, now to Thee.

I know I love Thee better
   Than any earthly joy,
For Thou hast given me the peace
   Which nothing can destroy.

I know that Thou art nearer still
   Than all this merry throng,
And sweeter is the thought of Thee
   Than any lovely song.

Thou hast put gladness in my heart,
   Then well may I be glad!
Without the secret of Thy love,
   I could not but be sad.

I bless Thee for these pleasant hours
   With sunny-hearted friends,

But more for this sweet moment's calm
   Thy loving-kindness sends.

O Master, gracious Master,
   What will Thy presence be,
If such a thrill of joy can crown
   One upward look to Thee?

'Tis ending now, that gentle song,
   And they will call for me;
They know the music I love best,—
   My song shall be for Thee!

For Thee, who hast so loved us,
   And whom, not having seen,
We love; on whom in all our joy,
   As in our grief, we lean.

Be near me still, and tune my notes,
   And make them sweet and strong,
To waft Thy words to many a heart
   Upon the wings of song.

I know that all will listen,
   For my very heart shall sing,
And it shall be Thy praise alone,
   My glorious Lord and King.

WHO WILL TAKE CARE OF ME?

WRITTEN FOR EMILY F. W. W. SNEPP

WHO will take care of me? darling, you say!
  Lovingly, tenderly watched as you are!
Listen! I give you the answer to-day,
  ONE who is never forgetful or far!

He will take care of you! all through the day,
  Jesus is near you to keep you from ill;
Walking or resting, at lessons or play,
  Jesus is with you and watching you still.

He will take care of you! all through the night,
  Jesus, the Shepherd, His little one keeps;
Darkness to Him is the same as the light;
  He never slumbers and He never sleeps.

He will take care of you! all through the year,
  Crowning each day with His kindness and love,
Sending you blessing and shielding from fear,
  Leading you on to the bright home above.

He will take care of you! yes, to the end!
  Nothing can alter His love to His own.
Darling, be glad that you have such a Friend,
  He will not leave you one moment alone!

BEGIN AT ONCE

BAND OF HOPE SONG

BEGIN at once! In the pleasant days,
　　While we are all together,
While we can join in prayer and praise,
While we can meet for healthful plays,
　　In the glow of summer weather.
Begin at once, with heart and hand,
And swell the ranks of our happy band.

Begin at once! For we do not know
　　What may befall to-morrow!
Many a tempter, many a foe
Lieth in wait where'er you go,
　　With the snare that leads to sorrow.
Begin at once! nor doubting stand,
But swell the ranks of our happy band.

Begin at once! There is much to do;
　　Oh, do not wait for others!
Join us to-day!—be brave and true;
Join us to-day!—there's room for you,
　　And a welcome from your brothers.
Begin at once! for the work is grand
That God has given to our happy band.

Begin at once! In the strength of God,
　　For that will never fail you!
Under His banner, bright and broad,
You shall be safe from fear and fraud,
　　And from all that can assail you.
Begin at once,—with resolute stand,
And swell the ranks of our happy band.

FILLING

Filled with all the fulness of God.—Ephesians 3:19.

I.
HOLY Father, Thou hast spoken
  Words beyond our grasp of thought,—
Words of grace and power unbroken,
  With mysterious glory fraught.

II.
Promise and command combining,
  Doubt to chase and faith to lift;
Self renouncing, all resigning,
  We would claim this mighty gift.

III.
Take us, Lord, oh, take us truly,
  Mind and soul and heart and will;
Empty us and cleanse us thoroughly,
  Then with all Thy fulness fill.

IV.
Lord, we ask it, hardly knowing
  What this wondrous gift may be;
But fulfil to overflowing,—
  Thy great meaning let us see.

V.
Make us in Thy royal palace
  Vessels worthy for the King;
From Thy fulness fill our chalice,
  From Thy never-failing spring.

VI.
Father, by this blessed filling,
  Dwell Thyself in us, we pray;
We are waiting, Thou art willing,
  Fill us with Thyself to-day!

MY MASTER

I love my master; . . . I will not go out free.
And he shall serve him for ever.—Exodus 21:5–6.

I.
I LOVE, I love my Master,
  I will not go out free,
For He is my Redeemer,
  He paid the price for me.

II.
I would not leave His service,
  It is so sweet and blest;
And in the weariest moments
  He gives the truest rest.

III.
I would not halve my service,
  His only it must be,—
His *only*, who so loved me
  And gave Himself for me.

IV.
My Master shed His life-blood
  My vassal life to win,
And save me from the bondage
  Of tyrant self and sin.

V.
He chose me for His service,
  And gave me power to choose
That blessed, "perfect freedom"
  Which I shall never lose:

VI.
For He hath met my longing
  With word of golden tone,
That I shall serve for ever
  Himself, Himself alone.

VII.

"Shall serve Him," hour by hour,
  For He will show me how;
My Master is fulfilling
  His promise even now!

VIII.

"Shall serve Him," and "for ever:"
  O hope most sure, most fair!
The perfect love outpouring
  In perfect service there!

IX.

Rejoicing and adoring,
  Henceforth my song shall be:
I love, I love my Master,
  I will not go out free!

THE MINISTRY OF SONG

In God's great field of labour
  All work is not the same;
He hath a service for each one
  Who loves His holy name.
And you, to whom the secrets
  Of all sweet sounds are known,
Rise up! for He hath called you
  To a mission of your own.
And, rightly to fulfil it,
  His grace can make you strong,
Who to your charge hath given
  The Ministry of Song.

Sing to the little children,
  And they will listen well;
Sing grand and holy music,
  For they can feel its spell.
Tell them the tale of Jephthah;
  Then sing them what he said,—
"Deeper and deeper still," and watch
  How the little cheek grows red,
And the little breath comes quicker:
  They will ne'er forget the tale,
Which the song has fastened surely,
  As with a golden nail.

I remember, late one evening,
  How the music stopped, for, hark!
Charlie's nursery door was open,
  He was calling in the dark,—
"Oh no! I am not frightened,
  And I do not want a light;
But I cannot sleep for thinking
  Of the song you sang last night.
Something about a 'valley,'
  And 'make rough places plain,'
And 'Comfort ye;' so beautiful!
  Oh, sing it me again!"

Sing at the cottage bedside;
    They have no music there,
And the voice of praise is silent
    After the voice of prayer.
Sing of the gentle Saviour
    In the simplest hymns you know,
And the pain-dimmed eye will brighten
    As the soothing verses flow.
Better than loudest plaudits
    The murmured thanks of such,
For the King will stoop to crown them
    With His gracious "Inasmuch."

Sing, where the full-toned organ
    Resounds through aisle and nave,
And the choral praise ascendeth
    In concord sweet and grave.
Sing, where the village voices
    Fall harshly on your ear;
And, while more earnestly you join,
    Less discord you will hear.
The noblest and the humblest
    Alike are "common praise,"
And not for human ear alone
    The psalm and hymn we raise.

Sing in the deepening twilight,
    When the shadow of eve is nigh,
And her purple and golden pinions
    Fold o'er the western sky.
Sing in the silver silence,
    While the first moonbeams fall;
So shall your power be greater
    Over the hearts of all.
Sing till you bear them with you
    Into a holy calm,
And the sacred tones have scattered
    Manna, and myrrh, and balm.

Sing! that your song may gladden;
    Sing like the happy rills,
Leaping in sparkling blessing

Fresh from the breezy hills.
Sing! that your song may silence
   The folly and the jest,
And the "idle word" be banished
   As an unwelcome guest.
Sing! that your song may echo
   After the strain is past,
A link of the love-wrought cable
   That holds some vessel fast.

Sing to the tired and anxious
   It is yours to fling a ray,
Passing indeed, but cheering,
   Across the rugged way.
Sing to God's holy servants,
   Weary with loving toil,
Spent with their faithful labour
   On oft ungrateful soil.
The chalice of your music
   All reverently bear,
For with the blessed angels
   Such ministry you share.

When you long to bear the Message
   Home to some troubled breast,
Then sing with loving fervour,
   "Come unto Him, and rest."
Or would you whisper comfort,
   Where words bring no relief,
Sing how "He was despised,
   Acquainted with our grief."
And, aided by His blessing,
   The song may win its way
Where speech had no admittance,
   And change the night to day.

Sing, when His mighty mercies
   And marvellous love you feel,
And the deep joy of gratitude
   Springs freshly as you kneel;
When words, like morning starlight,
   Melt powerless,—rise and sing!

And bring your sweetest music
   To Him, your gracious King.
Pour out your song before Him
   To whom our best is due;
Remember, He who hears your prayer
   Will hear your praises too.

Sing on in grateful gladness!
   Rejoice in this good thing
Which the Lord thy God hath given thee,
   The happy power to sing.
But yield to Him, the Sovereign,
   To whom all gifts belong,
In fullest consecration,
   Your Ministry of Song,
Until His mercy grant you
   That resurrection voice,
Whose only ministry shall be,
   To praise Him and rejoice.

HE IS THY LIFE

I.
JESUS, Thy life is mine!
Dwell evermore in me;
  And let me see
That nothing can untwine
  My life from Thine.

II.
Thy life in me be shown!
Lord, I would henceforth seek
  To think and speak
Thy thoughts, Thy words alone,
  No more my own.

III.
Thy love, Thy joy, Thy peace,
Continuously impart
  Unto my heart;
Fresh springs, that never cease,
  But still increase.

IV.
The blest reality
Of resurrection power,
  Thy Church's dower,
Life more abundantly,
  Lord, give to me!

V.
Thy fullest gift, O Lord,
Now at Thy feet I claim,
  Through Thy dear name!
And touch the rapturous chord
  Of praise forth poured.

VI.

Jesus, my life is Thine,
And evermore shall be
Hidden in Thee!
For nothing can untwine
Thy life from mine.

WITHOUT CAREFULNESS

I would have you without carefulness.—1 Corinthians 7:32.

I.

MASTER! how shall I bless Thy name
  For Thy tender love to me,
For the sweet enablings of Thy grace,
  So sovereign, yet so free,
That have taught me to obey Thy word
  And cast my care on Thee!

II.

They tell of weary burdens borne
  For discipline of life,
Of long anxieties and doubts,
  Of struggle and of strife,
Of a path of dim perplexities
  With fears and shadows rife.

III.

Oh, I have trod that weary path,
  With burdens not a few,
With shadowy faith that Thou would'st lead
  And help me safely through,
Trying to follow and obey,
  And bear my burdens too.

IV.

Master! dear Master, Thou didst speak,
  And yet I did not hear,
Or long ago I might have ceased
  From every care and fear,
And gone rejoicing on my way
  From brightening year to year.

V.

Just now and then some steeper slope
  Would seem so hard to climb,
That I *must* cast my load on Thee;

And I left it for a time,
And wondered at the joy at heart,
   Like sweetest Christmas chime.

VI.

A step or two on winged feet,
   And then I turned to share
The burden Thou hadst taken up
   Of ever-pressing care;
So what I would not leave with Thee
   Of course I had to bear.

VII.

At last Thy precious precepts fell
   On opened heart and ear,
A varied and repeated strain
   I could not choose but hear,
Enlinking promise and command,
   Like harp and clarion clear:

VIII.

"No anxious thought upon thy brow
   The watching world should see;
No carefulness! O child of God,
   For *nothing* careful be!
But cast thou *all* thy care on Him
   Who always cares for thee."

IX.

Did not Thy loving Spirit come
   In gentle, gracious shower,
To work Thy pleasure in my soul
   In that bright, blessed hour,
And to the word of strong command
   Add faith and will and power?

X.

It was Thy word, it was Thy will—
   That was enough for me!
Henceforth no care shall dim my trust,
   For all is cast on Thee;

Henceforth my inmost heart shall praise
  The grace that set me free.
XI.
And now I find Thy promise true,
  Of perfect peace and rest;
I cannot sigh—I can but sing
  While leaning on Thy breast,
And leaving everything to Thee,
  Whose ways are always best.

XII.
I never thought it could be thus,—
  Month after month to know
The river of Thy peace without
  One ripple in its flow;
Without one quiver in the trust,
  One flicker in its glow.

XIII.
Oh, Thou hast done far more for me
  Than I had asked or thought!
I stand and marvel to behold
  What Thou, my Lord, hast wrought,
And wonder what glad lessons yet
  I shall be daily taught.

XIV.
How shall I praise Thee, Saviour dear,
  For this new life so sweet,
For taking all the care I laid
  At Thy beloved feet,
Keeping Thy hand upon my heart
  To still each anxious beat!

XV.
I want to praise, with life renewed,
  As I never praised before;
With voice and pen, with song and speech,
  To praise Thee more and more,
And the gladness and the gratitude
  Rejoicingly outpour.

XVI.

I long to praise Thee more, and yet
    This is no care to me:
If Thou shalt fill my mouth with songs,
    Then I will sing to Thee;
And if my silence praise Thee best,
    Then silent I will be.

XVII.

Yet if it be Thy will, dear Lord,
    Oh, send me forth, to be
Thy messenger to careful hearts,
    To bid them taste and see
How good Thou art to those who cast
    All, all their care on Thee!

ONLY

I.

ONLY a mortal's powers,
　　Weak at their fullest strength;
Only a few swift-flashing hours,
　　Short at their fullest length.

II.

Only a page for the eye,
　　Only a word for the ear,
Only a smile, and by and by
　　Only a quiet tear.

III.

Only one heart to give,
　　Only one voice to use;
Only one little life to live,
　　And only one to lose.

IV.

Poor is my best, and small:
　　How could I dare divide?
Surely my Lord shall have it all,
　　He shall not be denied!

V.

All! for far more I owe
　　Than all I have to bring;
All! for my Saviour loves me so!
　　All! for I love my King!

VI.

All! for it is His own,
　　He gave the tiny store;
All! for it must be His alone;
　　All! for I have no more.

VII.

All! for the last and least
　　He stoopeth to uplift:
The altar of my great High Priest
　　Shall sanctify my gift.

124

TRIED, PRECIOUS, SURE

JESUS CHRIST
{
The Same yesterday, and to-day, and for ever.
—Hebrews 13:8.
A stone, a tried stone, a precious corner stone, a sure foundation.
—Isaiah 28:16.

I.

THROUGH the yesterday of ages,
  Jesus, Thou hast been The Same;
Through our own life's chequered pages,
  Still the one dear changeless name.
Well may we in Thee confide,
Faithful Saviour, proved and "TRIED!"

II.

Joyfully we stand and witness
  Thou art still to-day The Same;
In Thy perfect, glorious fitness,
  Meeting every need and claim.
Chiefest of ten thousand Thou!
Saviour, O most "PRECIOUS," now!

III.

Gazing down the far for ever,
  Brighter glows the one sweet Name
Stedfast radiance, paling never,
  Jesus, Jesus! still The Same.
Evermore "Thou shalt endure,"
Our own Saviour, strong and "SURE!"

VALIANT FOR THE TRUTH

Ye should earnestly contend for the faith which was once delivered unto the saints.—Jude 3.

UNFURL the Christian Standard! lift it manfully on high,
And rally where its shining folds wave out against the sky!
Away with weak half-heartedness, with faithlessness and fear!
Unfurl the Christian Standard, and follow with a cheer!

In God's own name we set it up, this banner brave and bright,
Uplifted for the cause of Christ, the cause of Truth and Right;
The cause that none can overthrow, the cause that must prevail,
Because the promise of the Lord can never, never fail!

Now, who is on the Lord's side, who? come, throng His battle-field;
Be strong, and show that ye are men! come forth with sword and shield!
What peace, while traitorous Evil stalks in false array of light?
What peace, while enemies of Christ are gathering for the fight?

Unfurl the Christian Standard, with firm and fearless hands!
For no pale flag of compromise with Error's legion bands,
And no faint-hearted flag of truce with Mischief and with Wrong,
Should lead the soldiers of the Cross, the faithful and the strong.

Unfurl the Christian Standard, and follow through the strife,
The noble army who have won the martyr's crown of life;
Our ancestors could die for Truth, could brave the deadly glow,
And shall we let the standard fall, and yield it to the foe?

But if ye dare not hold it fast, yours only is the loss,
For it *shall* be victorious, this Standard of the Cross!
It shall not suffer, though ye rest beneath your sheltering trees,
And cast away the victor's crown for love of timid ease.

The Lord of Hosts, in whom alone our weakness shall be strong,
Shall lead us on to conquest with a mighty battle song;
And soon the warfare shall be past, the glorious triumph won,
The kingdoms of this world *shall* be the kingdoms of His Son!

GROWING

I.

UNTO him that hath, Thou givest
Ever "more abundantly."
Lord, I live because Thou livest,
Therefore give more life to me;
Therefore speed me in the race;
Therefore let me grow in grace.

II.

Deepen all Thy work, O Master,
Strengthen every downward root,
Only do Thou ripen faster,
More and more, Thy pleasant fruit.
Purge me, prune me, self abase,
Only let me grow in grace.

III.

Jesus, grace for grace outpouring,
Show me ever greater things;
Raise me higher, sunward soaring,
Mounting as on eagle-wings.
By the brightness of Thy face,
Jesus, let me grow in grace.

IV.

Let me grow by sun and shower,
Every moment water me;
Make me really hour by hour
More and more conformed to Thee,
That Thy loving eye may trace,
Day by day, my growth in grace.

V.

Let me then be always growing,
Never, never standing still;
Listening, learning, better knowing
Thee and Thy most blessed will.
Till I reach Thy holy place,
Daily let me grow in grace.

BY THY CROSS AND PASSION

He hath given us rest by His sorrow, and life by His death.
—JOHN BUNYAN

I.

WHAT hast Thou done for me, O mighty Friend,
    Who lovest to the end!
Reveal Thyself, that I may now behold
    Thy love unknown, untold,
Bearing the curse, and made a curse for me,
That blessed and made a blessing I might be.

II.

Oh, Thou wast crowned with thorns, that I might wear
    A crown of glory fair;
"Exceeding sorrowful," that I might be
    Exceeding glad in Thee;
"Rejected and despised," that I might stand
Accepted and complete on Thy right hand.

III.

Wounded for my transgression, stricken sore,
    That I might "sin no more;"
Weak, that I might be always strong in Thee;
    Bound, that I might be free;
Acquaint with grief, that I might only know
Fulness of joy in everlasting flow.

IV.

Thine was the chastisement, with no release,
    That mine might be the peace;
The bruising and the cruel stripes were Thine,
    That healing might be mine;
Thine was the sentence and the condemnation,
Mine the acquittal and the full salvation.

V.

For Thee revilings, and a mocking throng,
    For me the angel-song;

For Thee the frown, the hiding of God's face,
      For me His smile of grace;
Sorrows of hell and bitterest death for Thee,
And heaven and everlasting life for me.

VI.

Thy cross and passion, and Thy precious death,
      While I have mortal breath,
Shall be my spring of love and work and praise,
      The life of all my days;
Till all this mystery of love supreme
Be solved in glory—glory's endless theme.

LIVE OUT THY LIFE WITHIN ME

Live out Thy life within me, O Jesus, King of kings!
Be Thou Thyself the answer to all my questionings;
Live out Thy life within me, in all things have Thy way!
I, the transparent medium, Thy glory to display.

The temple has been yielded, and purified of sin,
Let Thy Shekinah glory now shine forth from within,
And all the earth keep silence, the body henceforth be
Thy silent, gentle servant, moved only as by Thee.

Its members every moment held subject to Thy call,
Ready to have Thee use them, or not be used at all,
Held without restless longing, or strain, or stress, or fret,
Or chafings at Thy dealings, or thoughts of vain regret.

But restful, calm and pliant, from bend and bias free,
Awaiting Thy decision, when Thou hast need of me.
Live out Thy life within me, O Jesus, King of kings!
Be Thou the glorious answer to all my questionings.

ANOTHER FOR CHRIST

ANOTHER called, another brought, dear Master, to Thy feet!
Oh, where are words to tell the joy so wonderful and sweet!
Oh, where are words to give Thee thanks that Thou indeed hast heard,
That Thou hast proved and sealed anew Thy faithful promise-word!

We prayed so long, with fervent hope and patient faith, that she
With all her early wealth of love might give herself to Thee;
Well knowing that our prayer must be the echo of Thy will,
Itself the earnest and the pledge that Thou wilt all fulfil.

And now the prayer is turned to praise, and with the angel-throng,
Who even now are pouring forth a new and joyful song,
Our hearts ascend, our whispers blend, in deepest thrill of praise,
The happiest Alleluia-hymn that human heart can raise.

Oh, joy to know that Thou hast found Thy fair and weary dove,
Rejoicing o'er the wanderer now, and resting in Thy love,
That *Thou* art glad, that Thou hast seen the travail of Thy soul,
Thy blessed Name emblazoned on a new and living scroll!

O Master, blessed Master, it is hard indeed to know
That thousands round our daily path misunderstand Thee so!
Despised and rejected yet, no beauty they can see,
O King of glory and of grace, beloved Lord, in Thee!

Not even as a lovely song of pleasant voice appears
The story of Thy wondrous love in dull and drowsy ears;
'Tis nothing to the passers-by, who coldly turn aside,
That Thou hast poured Thy precious blood, that Thou wast crucified.

O Saviour, precious Saviour, come in all Thy power and grace,
And take away the veil that hides the glory of Thy face!
Oh, manifest the marvels of Thy tenderness and love,
And let Thy Name be blessed and praised all other names above.

Oh, vindicate Thyself, and show how perfect are Thy ways,
Untraceable, because too bright for weak and mortal gaze;
Shine forth, O Sun, and bid the scales of darkening evil fall,
Thou Altogether Lovely One, Thou glorious All-in-all!

Yet conquering Thy word goes forth on all-triumphant way!
"Ye *shall* be gathered one by one," 'tis true afresh to-day!

And so we hush the yearning cry, "How long, O Lord, how long?"
A sweet new token Thou hast given to change it into song.

So once again we praise Thee, with Thy holy ones above,
Because another heart has seen Thy great and mighty love;
Another heart will own Thee Lord, and worship Thee as King,
And grateful love and glowing praise and willing service bring.

Another voice to "tell it out" what great things Thou hast done,
Another life to live for Thee, another witness won,
Another faithful soldier on our Captain's side enrolled,
Another heart to read aright Thy heart of love untold!

CONFIDENCE

(IMPROMPTU ON THE ROAD TO WARWICK)

I.

In Thee I trust, on Thee I rest,
O Saviour dear, Redeemer blest!
No earthly friend, no brother knows
My weariness, my wants, my woes.
On Thee I call,
Who knowest all.
O Saviour dear, Redeemer blest,
In Thee I trust, on Thee I rest.

II.

Thy power, Thy love, Thy faithfulness,
With lip and life I long to bless.
Thy faithfulness shall be my tower,
My sun Thy love, my shield Thy power
In darkest night,
In fiercest fight.
With lip and life I long to bless
Thy power, Thy love, Thy faithfulness.

ACCEPTED

Accepted in the Beloved.—Ephesians 1:6.
Perfect in Christ Jesus.—Colossians 1:28.
Complete in Him.—Colossians 2:10.

ACCEPTED, Perfect, and Complete,
For God's inheritance made meet!
How true, how glorious, and how sweet!

In the Beloved—by the King
Accepted, though not anything
But forfeit lives had we to bring.

And Perfect in Christ Jesus made,
On Him our great transgressions laid,
We in His righteousness arrayed.

Complete in Him, our glorious Head,
With Jesus raised from the dead,
And by His mighty Spirit led!

O blessed Lord, is this for me?
Then let my whole life henceforth be
One Alleluia-song to Thee!

LIGHT AT EVENTIDE[1]

At evening time it shall be light.—Zechariah 14:7.

DEAR Lord, Thy good and precious Book seems written all for me;
Wherever I may open it, I find a word from Thee.
My eyes are dim, but this one verse is pillow for the night,
Thy promise that "At Evening Time it shall be" surely "light."

It was not always light with me; for many a sinful year
I walked in darkness, far from Thee; but Thou hast brought me near,
And washed me in Thy precious blood, and taught me by Thy grace,
And lifted up on my poor soul the brightness of Thy face.

My Saviour died in darkness that I might live in light,
He closed His eyes in death that mine might have the heavenly sight;
He gave up all His glory to bring it down to me,
And took the sinner's place that He the sinner's Friend might be.

His Spirit shines upon His Word, and makes it sweet indeed,
Just like a shining lamp held up beside me as I read;
And brings it to my mind again alone upon my bed,
Till all abroad within my heart the love of God is shed.

I've nearly passed the shadows and the sorrows here below;
A little while—a little while, and He will come, I know,
And take me to the glory that I think is very near,
Where I shall see Him face to face and His kind welcome hear.

And now my loving Jesus is my Light at Eventide,
The welcome Guest that enters in for ever to abide;
He never leaves me in the dark, but leads me all the way,—
So it *is* light at Evening Time, and soon it will be Day!

---

1 Written to accompany an engraving:—An old man, worn, but peaceful, sitting at his
cottage door in evening sunlight, with The Book on his knee.

NATIONAL HYMN

WRITTEN BY REQUEST TO MUSIC BY ROSSINI

O LORD most high,
Who art God and Father,
 Hear Thou our cry,
While Thy children gather!
  Lord of Peace, oh hearken,
  Though war-clouds darken!
  Do Thou our labours bless,
  And crown them with success!

Bend from Thy glory now,
Hear each suppliant vow!
And on our children pour
Blessings evermore.
  Guarded by Thee,
  England shall be
  Bright in Thy light,
  Strong in Thy might,
    Glorious and free!

Hero and saint,
  Victors at last,
Bid us not faint,
  But follow, follow fast.
  Make us, we pray,
  Loyal as they,
  Faithful and brave,
  Our country to save!

  When in the grim fight,
  Pierceth the dim light,
Through the cleft ranks that shall close no more,
  Fearfully flashing,
  Awfully crashing,
Death-furrows follow the cannon's roar,
  When wounded lie,
  Ready to die;
  When death is braved,
  That life may be saved;

Teach us to show
  Mercy with might,
Pardon the foe,
  Crown Thou the right!

Father, hear us!
Thou art near us!
Guard and cheer us
  By Thy strong hand!
Then Art resplendent,
Labour attendant,
  Shall bless our land!

Lord, bless the land we love,
  God save our Queen!

THERE IS MUSIC BY THE RIVER

THERE is music by the river,
   And music by the sea,
And music in the waterfall
   That gusheth glad and free.
There is music in the brooklet
   That singeth all alone,
There is music in the fountain
   With its silver-tinkling tone.

But the music of thy spirit
   Is sweeter far to me
Than the melody of rivers,
   Or the anthems of the sea.
Why should I dwell in silence
   When the music is so near
That may overflow my spirit
       So full, so clear!
          Oh! let me listen!

There is music in the forest,
   A myriad-voiced song;
And music on the mountains
   As the great winds rush along:
There is music in the gladness
   Of morning's merry light,
And in silence of the noontide,
   And in hush of starry night.

But a deeper, holier music
   Is the music of thy soul,
And I think the angels listen
   As its starry echoes roll.
Why should I dwell in silence
   When the music that is thine
May overflow my spirit
       And blend—with mine!
         Oh! let me listen!

A MERRIE CHRISTMAS

"A MERRIE Christmas" to you!
   For we serve the Lord with mirth,
And we carol forth glad tidings
   Of our holy Saviour's birth.
So we keep the olden greeting
   With its meaning deep and true,
And wish "a merrie Christmas"
   And a happy New Year to you!

Oh, yes! "a merrie Christmas,"
   With blithest song and smile,
Bright with the thought of Him who dwelt
   On earth a little while,
That we might dwell for ever
   Where never falls a tear:
So "a merrie Christmas" to you,
   And a happy, happy year!

THY FATHER WAITS FOR THEE

WANDERER from thy Father's home,
　So full of sin, so far away,
Wilt thou any longer roam?
　Oh, wilt thou not return to-day?
Wilt thou? Oh, He knows it all,
　Thy Father sees, He meets thee here!
Wilt thou? Hear His tender call,
　"Return, return!" while He is near.

He is here! His loving voice
　Hath reached thee, though so far away!
He is waiting to rejoice,
　O wandering one, o'er thee to-day.
Waiting, waiting to bestow
　His perfect pardon, full and free;
Waiting, waiting till thou know
　His wealth of love for thee, for thee!

Rise and go! Thy Father waits
　To welcome and receive and bless;
Thou shalt tread His palace gates
　In royal robe of righteousness.
Thine shall be His heart of love,
　And thine His smile, and thine His home,
Thine His joy, all joys above—
　O wandering child, no longer roam!

ENOUGH

I.

I AM so weak, dear Lord, I cannot stand
　　One moment without Thee!
But oh! the tenderness of Thine enfolding,
And oh! the faithfulness of Thine upholding,
And oh! the strength of Thy right hand!
　　That strength is enough for me!

II.

I am so needy, Lord, and yet I know
　　All fulness dwells in Thee;
And hour by hour that never-failing treasure
Supplies and fills, in overflowing measure,
My least, my greatest need; and so
　　Thy grace is enough for me!

III.

It is so sweet to trust Thy word alone:
　　I do not ask to see
The unveiling of Thy purpose, or the shining
Of future light on mysteries untwining:
Thy promise-roll is all my own,—
　　Thy word is enough for me!

IV.

The human heart asks love; but now I know
　　That my heart hath from Thee
All real, and full, and marvellous affection,
So near, so human; yet divine perfection
Thrills gloriously the mighty glow!
　　Thy love is enough for me!

V.

There were strange soul-depths, restless, vast, and broad,
　　Unfathomed as the sea;
An infinite craving for some infinite stilling;
But now Thy perfect love is perfect filling!
Lord Jesus Christ, my Lord, my God,
　　Thou, Thou art enough for me!

PRAYER BEFORE CHURCH

Lord, I am in Thy house of prayer,
Oh, teach me rightly how to pray;
Incline to me Thy gracious ear,
And listen, Lord, to what I say.

Give me, O Lord, a praying heart,
And also an attentive ear;
Help me to choose the better part,
And teach me Thee to love and fear.

A PRAYER

LORD, in mercy pardon me
All that I this day have done:
Sins of every kind 'gainst Thee,
O forgive them through Thy Son.

Make me, Jesus, like to Thee,
Gentle, holy, meek, and mild,
My transgressions pardon me,
O forgive a sinful child.

Gracious Spirit, listen Thou,
Enter in my willing heart,
Enter and possess it now,
Never, Lord, from me depart.

O eternal Three in One,
Condescend to bend Thine ear;
Help me still towards heaven to run,
Answer now my humble prayer.

THOUGHTS

On entering church when the sunshine streamed through the large window, so that its outline was completely lost in the overpowering brilliance.

OH, Thou, the Sun of Righteousness,
Whose bright rays every cloud dispel,
E'en yon fair brilliance is far less
Than that wherein Thou aye dost dwell.

Oh, Thou, my precious Saviour, shine
In all Thy radiance on my soul;
Oh, let me know what love is Thine,
Oh, let me reach this long-sought goal.

To me, to me Thy glory show,
Shall ever be my earnest prayer;
Grant me to leave the things below,
And in that perfect bliss to share,

Which to Thy faithful ones is given.
Oh, let Thy glory on me beam,
And let me taste the joys of heaven,
Before the close of life's strange dream.

Soon, Lord, reveal Thyself to me;
How long must I thus sadly wait?
My spirit yearns Thyself to see,
Oh, hear me in Thy mercy great!

"HE THAT OVERCOMETH"

He that overcometh, the same shall be clothed in white raiment; and I will not blot out his name out of the book of life, but I will confess his name before my Father, and before his angels.—Revelation 3:5.

"He that overcometh in the fight
Shall be clothed in raiment white and pure;
In the ever-blessed book of life
Shall his name eternally endure."

"When my Father on His dazzling throne
Sits, with myriad angels all around,
I'll confess his name, to men unknown;
Heaven and earth shall listen to the sound."

Who, with such a glorious end in view,
Would not in the heavenly conflict join?
Strange that willing soldiers are so few,
Strange so many faint, who once were Thine.

Oh, it is a service blest indeed!
Though the strife be long, the end is sure;
And our Leader gives to all who need
Grace that they may to the end endure.

'Neath Thy standard be my place, O Lord:
Grant me strength and grace, that I ere long
May obtain that rich and full reward.
Then, as conquering I sheath my sword,
Thou, my Captain, shall be all my song.

A SONG OF WELCOME

(FOR THE ST. NICHOLAS SUNDAY SCHOOL)

Oh God, with grateful hearts we come
   Thy goodness to adore,
While we our Pastor welcome home
   To England's happy shore.

For Thy delivering love we praise,
   And Thy restoring hand,—
Oh spare him yet for long, long days
   To this our little band.

Thy Spirit's fulness on him rest,
   Thy love his sunshine be!
And may he still, while doubly blest,
   A blessing be from Thee.

When the Chief Shepherd shall appear,
   May he receive, we pray,
A crown of glory bright and clear
   That fadeth not away.

THE LORD IS GRACIOUS

The Lord is gracious and full of compassion,
slow to anger and of great mercy.—Psalm 145:8.

THE Lord is gracious—full of grace
To those who seek through Christ His face;
O come then, sinner, taste and see
The fulness *of His love* for thee.

Full of compassion is His heart,
Each weary sigh, each rankling smart
Is known to Him whom we adore,
The Saviour who our sorrows bore.

To anger slow! though every hour
Provoking His destroying power;
How strange, such words of peace to give,
Through Him who died that we might live.

Great mercy! Yet another seal
To all His gracious words reveal;
Great mercy for the greatly stained,
For those who mercy long disdained.

We little know God's thoughts to man,
They are too great for us to scan:
Thou art too high and we too low,
The wonders of Thy love to know.

But crown Thy mercies, Lord, and send
Thy Spirit as our Teacher-Friend;
That we may see, and feel, and praise
The grace and love of all Thy ways!

THE SPIRIT PROCEEDING FROM THE FATHER

The Spirit proceeding from the Father and the Son.

O Spirit of our Triune Lord,
    Known by Thy might, unseen but felt,
Be Thy sweet influence now outpoured,
    With power to rouse, with love to melt.

O Holy One, who dost proceed
    Both from the Father and the Son,
Reveal to us our sin and need,
    And what our Saviour Christ hath done.

O Thou, whose love, exceeding great,
    Sent Thine own Son to bleed and die,
For Thy good Spirit's power we wait,
    Thy glorious grace to testify.

HYMN FOR IRELAND

The isles shall wait upon Me, and on Mine arm shall they trust.
—Isaiah 51:5.

FATHER, we would plead Thy promise, bending at Thy glorious throne,
That the isles shall wait upon Thee, trusting in Thine arm alone!
One bright isle we bring before Thee, while in faith Thy children pray
For a full and mighty blessing, with united voice to-day.

Gracious Saviour, look in mercy on this Island of the West,
Win the wandering and the weary with Thy pardon and Thy rest:
As the *only* Friend and Saviour let Thy blessed name be owned,
Who hast shed Thy blood most precious, and for ever hast atoned!

Blessed Spirit, lift Thy standard, pour Thy grace, and shed Thy light!
Lift the veil and loose the fetter; come with new and quickening might;
Make the desert places blossom, shower Thy sevenfold gifts abroad;
Make Thy servants wise and stedfast, valiant for the truth of God.

Triune God of grace and glory, be the isle for which we plead
Shielded, succoured with Thy blessing, strong in every hour of need;
Flooded with Thy truth and glory (glowing sunlight from above),
And encompassed with the ocean of Thine everlasting love.

Oh, surround Thy throne of power with Thine emerald bow of peace:
Bid the wailing, and the warring, and the wild confusion cease.
Thou remainest King for ever,—Thou shalt reign, and earth adore!
Thine the kingdom, Thine the power, Thine the glory evermore.

CHURCH MISSIONARY JUBILEE HYMN

He shall see of the travail of His soul, and shall be satisfied.
—Isaiah 53:11.

REJOICE with Jesus Christ to-day,
All ye who love His holy sway!
The travail of His soul is past,
He shall be satisfied at last.

Rejoice with Him, rejoice indeed,
For He shall see His chosen seed!
But ours the trust, the grand employ,
To work out this divinest joy.

Of all His own He loseth none,
They shall be gathered one by one;
He gathereth the smallest grain,
His travail shall not be in vain.

Arise and work! arise and pray
That He would haste the dawning day!
And let the silver trumpet sound,
Wherever Satan's slaves are found.

The vanquished foe shall soon be stilled,
The conquering Saviour's joy fulfilled,
Fulfilled in us, fulfilled in them,
His crown, His royal diadem.

Soon, soon our waiting eyes shall see
The Saviour's mighty Jubilee!
His harvest-joy is filling fast,
He shall be satisfied at last!

WHAT WILL YOU DO WITHOUT HIM?

I COULD not do without Him!
    Jesus is more to me
Than all the richest, fairest gifts
    Of earth could ever be.
But the more I find Him precious—
    And the more I find Him true—
The more I long for you to find
    What He can be to you.

You need not do without Him,
    For He is passing by,
He is waiting to be gracious,
    Only waiting for your cry;
He is waiting to receive you—
    To make you all His own!
Why will you do without Him,
    And wander on alone?

Why will you do without Him?
    Is He not kind indeed?
Did He not die to save you?
    Is He not all you need?
Do you not want a Saviour?
    Do you not want a Friend?
One who will love you faithfully,
    And love you to the end?

Why will you do without Him?
    The word of God is true,
The world is passing to its doom—
    And you are passing too.
It may be no to-morrow
    Shall dawn on you or me;
Why will you run the awful risk
    Of all eternity?

What will you do without Him,
    In the long and dreary day
Of trouble and perplexity,
    When you do not know the way,

And no one else can help you,
   And no one guides you right,
And hope comes not with morning,
   And rest comes not with night?

You could not do without Him,
   If once He made you see
The fetters that enchain you,
   Till He hath set you free:
If once you saw the fearful load
   Of sin upon your soul—
The hidden plague that ends in death,
   Unless He makes you whole.

What will you do without Him
   When death is drawing near?
Without His love—the only love
   That casts out every fear;
When the shadow-valley opens,
   Unlighted and unknown,
And the terrors of its darkness
   Must all be passed alone!

What will you do without Him,
   When the great white throne is set,
And the Judge who never can mistake,
   And never can forget,—
The Judge whom you have never here
   As Friend and Saviour sought,
Shall summon you to give account
   Of deed and word and thought?

What will you do without Him,
   When He hath shut the door,
And you are left outside, because
   You would not come before?
When it is no use knocking,
   No use to stand and wait,
For the word of doom tolls through your heart,
   That terrible "Too late!"

You *cannot* do without Him
   There is no other Name

By which you ever *can* be saved,
    No way, no hope, no claim!
Without Him—everlasting loss
    Of love, and life, and light!
Without Him—everlasting woe,
    And everlasting night.

But with Him—oh! *with Jesus!*
    Are any words so blest?
With Jesus, everlasting joy
    And everlasting rest!
With Jesus,—all the empty heart
    Filled with His perfect love;
With Jesus,—perfect peace below,
    And perfect bliss above.

Why should you do without Him?
    It is not yet too late;
He has not closed the day of grace,
    He has not shut the gate.
He calls you!—hush! He calls you!
    He would not have you go
Another step without Him,
    Because He loves you so.

He would not do without you!
    He calls and calls again—
"Come unto Me! Come unto Me!"
    Oh, shall He call in vain?
He wants to have you with Him;
    Do you not want Him too?
You cannot do without Him,
    And He wants—even you.

"FORGIVEN—EVEN UNTIL NOW"

Pardon, I beseech thee, the iniquity of this people according unto the greatness of thy mercy, and as thou hast forgiven this people, from Egypt even until now.—Numbers 14:19.

FOR NEW YEAR'S DAY 1879

"Thou hast forgiven—even until now!"
    We bless Thee, Lord, for this,
And take Thy great forgiveness as we bow
    In depth of sorrowing bliss;
While over all the long, regretful past
This veil of wondrous grace Thy sovereign hand doth cast.

"Forgiven until now!" For Jesus died
    To take our sins away;
His Blood was shed, and still the infinite tide
    Flows full and deep to-day.
He paid the debt; we own it, and go free!
The cancelled bond is cast in Love's unfathomed sea.

"Forgiven until now!" For God is true,
    Faithful and just is He!
Forgiving, cleansing, making all things new!
    "Who is a God like Thee?"
O precious blood of Christ, that saves and heals,
While all its cleansing might the Holy Ghost reveals.

Yes, "even until now!" And so we stand,
    Forgiven, loved, and blessed;
And, covered in the shadow of God's hand,
    Believing, are at rest.
The one great load is lifted from the soul,
That henceforth on the Lord all burdens we may roll.

Yes, "even until now!" Then let us press
    With free and willing feet
Along the King's highway of holiness,
    Until we gain the street
Of golden crystal, praising purely when
We see our pardoning Lord; forgiven until then!

ASKING

*If ye then, being evil, know how to give good gifts unto
your children: how much more shall your heavenly Father
give the Holy Spirit to them that ask him?*—Luke 11:13.

O HEAVENLY Father, Thou hast told
Of a Gift more precious than pearls and gold:
A Gift that is free to every one,
Through Jesus Christ, Thy only Son:
    For His sake, give it to me.

Oh, give it to me! for Jesus said,
That a father giveth his children bread,
And how much more Thou wilt surely give
The Gift by which the dead shall live!
    For Christ's sake, give it to me.

If Thou hast said it, I must believe
It is only "ask" and I shall receive;
If Thou hast said it, it must be true,
And there's nothing else for me to do!
    For Christ's sake, give it to me.

So I come and ask, because my need
Is very great and real indeed.
On the strength of Thy word I come and say,
Oh, let Thy word come true to-day!
    For Christ's sake, give it to me!

LOVE FOR LOVE

And we have known and believed the love that God hath to us. God is love; and he that dwelleth in love dwelleth in God, and God in him.—1 John 4:16.

KNOWING that the God on high,
    With a tender Father's grace,
Waits to hear your faintest cry,
    Waits to show a Father's face,—
Stay and think!—oh, should not you
Love this gracious Father too?

Knowing Christ was crucified,
    Knowing that He loves you now
Just as much as when He died
    With the thorns upon His brow,—
Stay and think!—oh, should not you
Love this blessed Saviour too?

Knowing that a Spirit strives
    With your weary, wandering heart,
Who can change the restless lives,
    Pure and perfect peace impart,—
Stay and think!—oh, should not you
Love this loving Spirit too?

www.ingramcontent.com/pod-product-compliance
Lightning Source LLC
Chambersburg PA
CBHW070836100426
42813CB00003B/638